HOW TO SOLVE
(just about)
ANY
PROBLEM

TIMELESS PRACTICES
FOR SOLVING
PROBLEMS BETTER

GREG Z. FAINBERG

Copyright © 2009

ISBN No: 9780620439329

First published in 2009
by CEXINO

Greg Z. Fainberg Contact Details

Mobile: +27 84 555 9581
E-mail: zwif@cexino.com
Online: http://www.cexino.com

Cover Design by: Wouter Reinders
First Printed by: Mega Digital
Online: http://www.megadigital.co.za

DEDICATION

This book is dedicated to all people looking to make a serious change in their life for the better. This is a self help manual that gives the essential practical information and insights about this important life skill and makes it easy for you to just pick it up and get going. Whatever challenges and problems you are facing in life, this book will serve as a roadmap to structure your thinking and give you confidence to get where you want to go. So many of our problems can so easily be dealt with but we either avoid them, run away from them, deny them or even curse them. This book will assist you in addressing your problems head on and help you create the progress and success that you are looking for. I hope you enjoy it and I wish you all the success in your future.

GREG Z. FAINBERG

Simmy

*"When you change
the way you look at things
the things you look at change"*

CONTENTS

FOREWORD

"This is a great truth, one of the greatest truths. It is a great truth because once we truly see this truth, we transcend it. Once we truly know that life is difficult - once we truly understand and accept it - then life is no longer difficult. Because once it is accepted, the fact that life is difficult no longer matters"

M. Scott Peck
from The Road Less Travelled

What makes life difficult is the problems we all face at different stages of our lives. Just knowing that we have a structure and set of tools to solve any problem, reduces our feelings of anxiety and frustration. Everything seems easier. Whether you are facing a personal problem, or solving an organisational issue, this book will make it easy for you to be successful. Cooking up a solution to a problem means more than simply following a recipe. The problem solver's flair (his courage, passion, beliefs, and way of working), will affect the flavour of his dish.

So in Part 2, Greg covers the characteristics of a powerful problem solver. Then in Part 3 to 7, he provides easy to follow recipes for solving 'just about any problem' from start to finish. And if that isn't enough, he packs in extra value. Part 8 provides extra checklists and templates. This gem of a book, is filled to the brim with life wisdoms, simple advice, practical tools, and inspirational quotes about problem solving.

With this simple, practical book, individuals, team leaders, project managers, middle managers, training departments and business schools have a guide for solving (just about) any problem.

RUTH TEARLE

CHANGE DESIGNS

WWW.CHANGEDESIGNS.CO.ZA

*"An hour
of thinking
may equal as
much effort as
ten hours of
physical work"*

WHY YOU SHOULD READ THIS BOOK?

"A good head and a good heart are always a formidable combination"

- Nelson Mandela

Today's world is full of problems. Every single human being is faced with problems on a daily basis. Some problems are big, and some are small. Some are simple and some are more complicated. Some take a few minutes to solve whilst others take years to address. Effective problem solving is a fundamental necessity for every human being. Being able to solve problems better would make anyone and everyone much more effective in whatever field they are in. The sad reality of humanity is that many people just don't know how to solve their problems effectively.

The results of poor problem solving are riddled in the pages of history books and are clearly visible in today's reality. To be perfectly blunt, the reason for so much sadness, misery, despair, poverty, war, hatred, malice and frustration really comes down to humanity's inability to think effectively or creatively and due to poor problem solving. And, if people were taught how to think effectively and to solve problems better they would be far more creative and better able to make smarter, more effective decisions. There would certainly be less suffering in the world.

Just imagine how much more productive and effective we can be as a race if we only learn how to address and solve our problems better (individually and together). Ironically, problem solving and decision making skills are not even taught in most schools and universities.

"Think before you Act"

The value of thinking (both creative and critical) in today's society is highly unappreciated. Not enough emphasis is placed on teaching people to think effectively especially from a young age. Religions, philosophies, cultures, families and education systems that are meant to fulfil this role, do far too little to encourage this essential life skill.

Teaching people to think effectively, solve their problems and make better decisions is such a necessary if not one of the most important enterprises in the world today. No matter what problems you are facing, the ability to structure your thinking in such a way that leads you to a better result, is an essential and invaluable skill.

"Look before you Leap"

This book will provide you with tools, checklists and insights that are easy, practical and applicable to deal with just about any problem. It will guide you to take effective action that is mindful and considerate. No matter what problems you are dealing with, this book will help you address them more effectively.

I trust that by the end of this book you not only become a better problem solver but help others including your children, family, friends and peers to become better problem solvers as well.

"Thoughts become words,
words become actions,
actions become habits,
habits become character,
character becomes destiny"

THIS BOOK WILL TEACH YOU:

1. To understand what problems are and why problem solving is so important now more than ever

2. To adopt a proactive, mindful, considerate and positive approach to problem solving

3. To understand and adopt the characteristics of effective problem solving

4. To understand how to define problems clearly and to recognise different perspectives

5. To understand the root causes of problems, the forces at play and the power of serenity

6. To learn how to think more effectively and creatively and to generate new or improved ideas

7. To learn how to sort through, evaluate and select the best ideas and make better decisions

8. To design effective action plans to help guide you in solving problems

9. To recognise what to avoid when it comes to solving problems

10. To use powerful tools, templates, techniques and insights to address and solve just about any problem

THE GENERAL STATE
OF PROBLEM SOLVING

"Too many problem-solving sessions become battlegrounds where decisions are made based on power rather than intelligence"

- Margaret J Wheatley

What most people tend to do when faced with problems is jump straight into solution mode and then evaluation mode and then start to argue about the possibilities. They have not even diagnosed the problem effectively enough and they are already looking for solutions. When people solve problems, they also get their egos involved. This is a mistake of cosmic proportions, because ego takes focus away from the problem at hand and puts it on the individual and on being right for the sake of ego and not being right for its own sake. Since people don't like to admit when they are wrong they begin to argue or fight.

In group problem solving what would have been a session that addresses a problem or a challenge directly, becomes an ego battle of who is right and wrong, who will win or lose, and who will look the best in front of the boss, teacher, friend or crowd. This is an old mentality that needs to be removed from the current way of thinking and solving problems. The world of today is far more complicated than it has ever been. It is faster. It is more competitive, the opportunities are infinite, and the complexities are profound. Our heads are spinning out of control and our sanity and morality is tested daily. Problem-solving and good quality thinking are (now more than ever) essential skills that you have to harness in order to become more effective and successful in this day and age. The good news is that problem-solving and good quality thinking are easy to understand and achieve but take a lifetime of practice, refinement and application. You have to learn to be mindful of your thinking, actions and consequences of those actions.

"Start to be right for 'Right' sake and not your ego or pride sake"

> *"Problems can not be solved by thinking within the framework in which they were created"*
>
> - Albert Einstein

SO WHAT IS A PROBLEM ANYWAY?

"A problem is the difference between what you've got and what you want"

- Peter Honey

If you think about it, everything you do is a problem waiting to be solved. But what is a problem? How do you understand the word *problem*? The Oxford English dictionary defines this word as *a difficult situation that needs to be resolved* another definition of a problem is *something hard to understand or do, a dilemma, a question, puzzle or an obstacle*. The world is full of problems. They are everywhere and will always exist. When you face any problem you have got to keep your head up and your eyes and ears open. Like the Ostrich, we shove our head in the ground and do the opposite.

We don't listen, we lose our cool, we panic, we worry, we get anxious, we get angry and depressed. These are not effective methods to solving problems and yet so many people use them. To be a successful problem solver, you need to think holistically and become mindful of yourself and your approach.

"I believe that if you show people the problems and you show them the solutions they will be moved to act"

- Bill Gates

We deal with problems every day, here are some of the typical examples:

- ✿ Acquiring a skill
- ✿ Becoming more confident
- ✿ Becoming more creative
- ✿ Becoming more motivated
- ✿ Becoming more objective and rational
- ✿ Choosing who to be with in a relationship
- ✿ Dealing with change and risks
- ✿ Dealing with crime
- ✿ Dealing with emergencies
- ✿ Dealing with misunderstandings
- ✿ Dealing with negative or difficult people
- ✿ Deciding where to go for dinner
- ✿ Finding a better route or path
- ✿ Fixing or renewing something
- ✿ Getting a better job
- ✿ Getting over a loss
- ✿ Improving health and education
- ✿ Improving the quality of life
- ✿ Learning something new
- ✿ Learning to control yourself
- ✿ Learning to forgive yourself and others
- ✿ Learning to manage your time better
- ✿ Making more money
- ✿ Making better decisions
- ✿ Overcoming a difficult obstacle
- ✿ Overcoming anger and negativity
- ✿ Overcoming relationship difficulties
- ✿ Saving and investing for the future
- ✿ Solving an equation and passing a test
- ✿ Solving hunger problems
- ✿ Speaking better in public

WHAT CAUSES
YOUR PROBLEMS?

"When solving problems, dig at the roots instead of just hacking at the leaves"

- Anthony J. D'Angelo

There are many causes to problems. A problem may be caused due to poor planning, poor communication, poor values, poor thinking, poor logic, poor perception, poor learning, poor action or poor intent. Problems exist and will continue to for as long as humans do. The challenge is to become more effective at addressing, solving and preventing them. The more mindful and aware you can become the better. The following section provides a list of the typical causes of problems. Consider where they pertain to you and reflect on where you should improve your thinking and behaviour.

TYPICAL CAUSES OF PROBLEMS

- ✘ Analysis paralysis - not taking action
- ✘ Being inconsiderate of others or the environment
- ✘ Being passive and not proactive
- ✘ Being too slow and wasting in general
- ✘ Bias and lack of fairness
- ✘ Blowing things out of proportion and being too excessive
- ✘ Corruption, injustice, crime and lack of civility
- ✘ Dealing with the symptoms and not the causes of problems
- ✘ Delusion - not acknowledging reality objectively
- ✘ Disrespectful behaviour, being false and having no integrity
- ✘ Failing to consider all the factors
- ✘ Failing to learn from the past or history
- ✘ Failing to plan and poorly set and acted upon goals
- ✘ Failing to take responsibility and action
- ✘ Failing to draw on experts and professionals
- ✘ Fear, laziness and procrastination
- ✘ Fuelling and not addressing bad habits
- ✘ Having low self esteem and being dependant
- ✘ Having low standards and low quality
- ✘ Inability to distinguish facts from fiction
- ✘ Insufficient creativity, options or ideas
- ✘ Lack of confidence and self esteem
- ✘ Lack of freedom and the presence of oppression
- ✘ Lack of mindfulness of short and long term consequences
- ✘ Lack of morality or just plain negativity
- ✘ Lack of motivation and perfectionism
- ✘ Lack of or not enough information and knowledge
- ✘ Lack of patience and serenity
- ✘ Lack of resources - time, money, skills, equipment
- ✘ Lack of self control and being irresponsible
- ✘ Lack of trust and trustworthiness
- ✘ Lack of vision, discipline and perseverance
- ✘ Lying and not keeping promises

- ✗ Making too many assumptions without checking
- ✗ Not asking (enough) questions
- ✗ Not being confident
- ✗ Not being organized or prepared
- ✗ Not negotiating effectively
- ✗ Not enough balance
- ✗ Not checking if work is up to standard
- ✗ Not considering all factors and jumping to conclusions
- ✗ Not having a backup plan
- ✗ Not including all necessary parties, groups or individuals
- ✗ Not reading the instructions, directions or prescriptions
- ✗ Not taking action
- ✗ Not willing to be helpful
- ✗ Over complicating issues unnecessarily
- ✗ Poor analysis and evaluation of information
- ✗ Poor communication or misunderstanding
- ✗ Poor emotional intelligence and emotions out of control
- ✗ Poor focus or concentration
- ✗ Poor health habits
- ✗ Poor listening and misunderstanding
- ✗ Poor memory and leaving things for the last minute
- ✗ Poor objectivity, judgement, logic and reason
- ✗ Poor or limited perception of a situation
- ✗ Rudeness, prejudice and having double standards
- ✗ Sacrifice long term for short term decisions
- ✗ Solving the wrong problem
- ✗ Stupid rules or policies that are no longer applicable
- ✗ Substituting action with wishes, hopes and prayers
- ✗ Taking uncalculated risks
- ✗ Taking things out of context
- ✗ Trying to harm another or spreading harmful gossip
- ✗ Unreasonable and unrealistic expectations
- ✗ Violence, crime and violating human rights
- ✗ Wanting to be right for ego sake not for right sake

SO WHAT CAN YOU DO ABOUT PROBLEMS?

"In order to solve or prevent any problem you must first acknowledge its existence"

Whether you realise it or not, you are always addressing problems. The difference between successful and unsuccessful problem solving lies in being proactive and mindful. Poor problem solving is usually the result of being reactive, making snap judgements, not focusing or addressing the problem objectively, panicking and losing your temper. The following lists depict the typical ways you can choose to solve your current problems. As you will notice, some of the methods will help reach positive or productive results and other methods will help you realise negative results. The choice is yours.

Consider a problem in your life that you are currently facing. Look at the list below and consider the method you are currently choosing to use. Is it effective? Is it providing you with the results you are looking for? The following are the methods:

1. UNDERSTAND THE PROBLEM CLEARLY, FACE IT, GET ALL THE INFORMATION, GET CREATIVE, SOLVE IT!

- ✓ Be objective, reasonable, realistic and positive
- ✓ Focus, address it directly and get all the information
- ✓ Understand where you are now in relation to where you want to be and define criteria for success clearly
- ✓ Understand the problem clearly, understand its root causes and understand all the forces at play
- ✓ Practice serenity, focus your energy on what you can change and take full responsibility to do it
- ✓ Consider all stakeholders interests, get creative and generate alternative ideas to address the problem
- ✓ Choose the alternatives that best meet your criteria for success within your limitations and boundaries
- ✓ Communicate clearly and exercise discipline
- ✓ Write a plan with dates and deadlines and take action
- ✓ Monitor changes, revise or change direction if necessary
- ✓ Learn from mistakes and failures for the future

ALTERNATIVELY YOU CAN...

2. Fight because you have no choice but to defend yourself

3. Fight and argue unnecessarily, be angry, and shout

4. Panic, be anxious and lose control and your temper

5. Be negative, sad, scared, depressed and run away

6. Be irresponsible, throw caution to the wind and ignore the consequences of your actions

7. Procrastinate, be lazy and leave it to the last minute

8. Wish, hope and pray that the problem disappears on its own by some miracle

9. Fantasize and dream about a better future but don't take any responsibility to do anything about it and leave it up to somebody else, a higher power or chance

10. Deny, ignore or avoid it - just pretend it's not there

11. Jump to conclusions and make assumptions immediately without questioning or thinking

12. Just complain and cry but don't do anything about it

*"Be part of the solution
not part of the problem"*

"Frustration and insanity come from doing the same thing over and over again and expecting a different result"

WHAT IF THE WORLD HAD BETTER PROBLEM SOLVERS?

"Wealth is the product of man's capacity to think"

- Ayn Rand

Just imagine what the world would be like if there was better problem solving. It would be a completely different world. So many of the problems experienced today are simply the result of poor thinking and poor problem solving taking place. Whether it is done by a child, parent, teacher, student, husband, wife, banker, lawyer, doctor, shopkeeper, manager, scientist or the president. If the skills of effective problem solving were promoted and practiced it would be a better world to live in. Some of the specific changes you can expect in a world where people solve problems better would include:

"Imagine all the people living life in peace"

\- John Lennon

IF THE WORLD HAD BETTER PROBLEM SOLVERS...

- ✿ Accomplish your goals and dreams faster
- ✿ Actions taken would be to benefit and not harm
- ✿ Awareness of short and long term consequences
- ✿ Better and improved growth and development
- ✿ Better business decisions that lead to success
- ✿ Better communication of information
- ✿ Better decisions taken (for the longer term)
- ✿ Better planning and pre-cautions taken
- ✿ Better relationships at home and work
- ✿ Better standards and a better quality of life
- ✿ Civility, morality, rationality and justice
- ✿ Eliminate hate, violence, propaganda, and arrogance
- ✿ Environmentally friendly and responsible decisions
- ✿ Have higher self-esteem and confidence
- ✿ Improved quality of thinking
- ✿ Lead a more responsible life
- ✿ Less corruption, violence, prejudice and hatred
- ✿ More consideration and respect of self and others
- ✿ More creativity and innovation
- ✿ More honesty, trustworthiness, integrity, and responsibility
- ✿ More quality, growth and development
- ✿ More responsible citizens and leaders
- ✿ More safety and security
- ✿ Resolve and negotiate conflicts more effectively
- ✿ Save more time and waste less
- ✿ The ability to change faster and more effectively
- ✿ The ability to create more happiness and peace
- ✿ The ability to generate solutions faster
- ✿ The ability to minimize or eliminate conflict

CURRENT AND FUTURE THREATS TO EFFECTIVE PROBLEM SOLVING

"All that is necessary for the triumph of evil is that good men do nothing"

- Edmund Burke

We live in a world where science and technology are advancing rapidly. Yet the quality of our social problem solving and thinking are still not sufficiently emphasized. Families still have the same old arguments. You still see mediocre social behaviour such as bullying in schools and organizations and at the extreme violence and murder. Corruption and crime are virtually everywhere. In a world where science and technology capacity is so useful to help us solve our daily problems, we still employ such backward mindless behaviours to harm one another that at the end result in mediocrity.

"While civilization has been improving our houses, it has not equally improved the men who are to inhabit them... improved means to unimproved ends"

- Henry David Thoreau

If individuals (especially children) are not taught to think effectively then society suffers terribly. Wars, violence, hatred and propaganda are the result. What kind of world are we preparing for future generations? Good thinking and problem solving need to become essential skills to learn and practice in order to prevent future generations suffering our poor past and present thinking. Some of the key threats include:

- ✗ Critical and creative thinking not taught, encouraged or practiced enough in schools, universities, work environments, families, cultural and religious groups

- ✗ Propaganda, brainwashing, dishonesty and lack of morality

- ✗ The power of the media to distort reality and spread lies or partial truths that are inconsistent, biased and irrational

- ✗ Bullying, corruption, violence, intimidation, double standards, inconsideration, rudeness, racism, sexism and harmful intent in private and public organizations

- ✗ Not learning from or completely ignoring history's lessons

- ✗ Popular (!) social and religious leaders, fanatics and fundamentalists irresponsibly promoting blind following and faith, and not taking personal responsibility for your life

- ✗ Lack of respect for human rights, defamation of character, hate and employing the 'might is right' attitude

ARE YOU TREATING OR PREVENTING PROBLEMS

*"Intellectuals solve problems,
geniuses prevent them"*

- Albert Einstein

Often some of the biggest causes of problems occur, and continue to do so, when we only address the symptoms of a problem but not address the cause. The results of this are (as can be expected) that we tend to have the same (or similar) problem, issue or situation occurring over and over again. But why do we not just treat the cause of our problems? The answer is mostly due to poor longer term thinking and laziness. Dealing with problems that are right in front of our face is 'easier' in the short term but not sustainable in the longer term.

If you get sick, the conventional way to address this is to consult with a doctor and to get the best available medicine or treatment. However if you don't take into account what has caused the disease (or problem) in the first place, learn from it and take necessary actions to prevent it from happening again next time you can be drowned in this problem for a very long time.

This same principle applies to human relationships. If a couple has an argument and the manner to resolve it is to simply kiss and make up, that may have solved the problem this time, but has not necessarily addressed why the couple has originally argued which may result in the couples' continued arguing over and over again about the same issues for a long time.

"Prevention is better than cure"

CHECKLIST FOR PREVENTING PROBLEMS:

✓ Ask what is causing the problem

✓ Consider if the problem you are facing is something you have faced before and ask why is this happening again

✓ Think about the future and what possible future scenarios may occur and work a way to address each possibility

✓ When looking for advice from experts make sure you share not only the symptoms of the problem but also the situations you are in and your behaviour lifestyle in order for them to get a better sense of the cause of the problem and if it has something to do with your lifestyle

✓ Consider your bad habits and how they are contributing to the problem

✓ Take full responsibility not just for addressing the problem but focus on preventing it as well

✓ Learn from your (and others) past mistakes. It is silly to make mistakes if you can learn from the mistakes of others and the past

✓ Consider the realistic 'what if' scenarios and take responsibility to address and prevent each one

✓ Don't leave things to chance

✓ What can you do to prevent the problem in future

ATTITUDES IN PROBLEM SOLVING

"How you think about a problem is more important than the problem itself, so always think positively"

- Norman Vincent Peale

Whatever problem you are dealing with it is always a good idea to adopt a positive attitude. An attitude is defined in the dictionary as *a way of thinking or behaving*. Even if the problem is a tough one it doesn't help you to be negative when you address it. Adopting a negative attitude to solve any problem will simply serve to drain your energy and motivation. Adopting a negative attitude will make you feel doubt, fear, stress, anxiety, anger, defeat and depression before you even begin addressing the problem.

BE MINDFUL AND AVOID THESE NEGATIVE ATTITUDES:

- ✗ I have to be right and can't be wrong
- ✗ I don't feel like it or maybe later or why bother trying
- ✗ I am just not good enough or never will be
- ✗ I always have to be perfect or I might as well not bother
- ✗ Not another problem or why or poor me
- ✗ It just can't be done or I can't succeed
- ✗ It's just the way I am and always will be
- ✗ I am not creative or can't think creatively
- ✗ I am only happy when others like, love or agree with me
- ✗ I am only happy when I win and others lose
- ✗ I just don't believe in myself or I'm worthless
- ✗ I'm not a child anymore or I'm afraid
- ✗ What will other people think about me
- ✗ I like things as they are or it's just the way it is
- ✗ What if I fail or make a mistake
- ✗ There's no other way or there's no hope
- ✗ It's my way or the highway

So make a mental note to adopt a positive attitude the next problem you address. Next time you catch yourself in a negative state, replace your negative attitude with a positive one. Practice the attitudes in the following list.

Positive Attitudes

- ✓ I am creative, objective and positive
- ✓ I am full of potential and energy
- ✓ I am loving, worthy of love and love myself
- ✓ I am grateful for all I have now
- ✓ I am powerful, gifted and full of potential
- ✓ I am full of energy and live each day to the maximum
- ✓ I can succeed if I put my mind to it and persevere
- ✓ I don't have to be perfect ONLY the best I can be
- ✓ I am confident and really do believe in myself
- ✓ I can achieve anything I put my mind to within reason
- ✓ I am amazing because there is no one else like me
- ✓ I am great and I want to be better
- ✓ I am not afraid to fail because it is part of life and learning
- ✓ I am ok with making mistakes as long as I don't repeat them
- ✓ I am not afraid of my own greatness
- ✓ Everything I experience is there to teach me
- ✓ I take full responsibility for my thoughts and actions
- ✓ Yes I can if I take responsibility and it's reasonable!
- ✓ I CHOOSE to be positive and to detach from negativity

*"Hold a funeral for I Can't
and say hello to I Can"*

WHAT'S THE MIND SET OF GOOD PROBLEM SOLVERS

"It is what a man thinks of himself that really determines his fate"

- Henry David Thoreau

P roblem solving is a process. If you learn the process you will get better at it. However it is also important to take note of the characteristics and mind set of effective problem solving as they will guide and support you. Just like an athlete who practices discipline, good problem solvers practice these characteristics in their everyday lives to get better and as a result constantly improve themselves. They understand that by keeping these characteristics alive in mind and heart, they will solve their problems more efficiently and effectively. The list of good problem solving characteristics follows.

CHARACTERISTICS OF GOOD PROBLEM SOLVERS:

- ✿ They are thoughtful and mindful
- ✿ They introspect on beliefs and values
- ✿ Logical, rational, objective, moral and have good judgement
- ✿ They are creative and can visualize
- ✿ They are considerate and genuine
- ✿ They are not shy about asking questions
- ✿ They tolerate mistakes, failure and constantly learn
- ✿ They exercise serenity and understand all the forces
- ✿ They are emotionally intelligent and independent
- ✿ They are inspired, optimistic and motivated
- ✿ They have a good sense of humour
- ✿ They manage priorities, time and are organized
- ✿ They are disciplined and patient
- ✿ They can build scenarios
- ✿ They have courage and confidence
- ✿ They are responsible, trustworthy, have integrity and choose
- ✿ They can change and adapt quickly
- ✿ They communicate clearly and listen
- ✿ They can overcome negativity and detach
- ✿ They show empathy and forgiveness
- ✿ They can negotiate effectively

It is not good enough to say you have these characteristics. You need to be mindful of your thinking and problem solving constantly. You need to practice, these characteristics every day until they become second nature to you. It doesn't matter what kind of problem you are dealing with, if you apply these principle characteristics you will be able to address any problem better.

The following section takes a closer look at these characteristics, what you should do to make them a part of your life and how to use them in problem solving.

"Hot heads and cold hearts
never solved anything"

- Billy Graham

THEY ARE THOUGHTFUL AND MINDFUL

"The empires of the future, are the empires of the mind"

- Winston Churchill

Thinking is humanity's most powerful ability. The ability to think propels us forward as a race, and precisely the lack of it that keeps us backward, irrational, foolish, or violent. Consider history for a moment. Consider the dark ages, the First and Second World Wars (And all wars in general), economic meltdowns, social and civil collapses. Think of any other negative historical event. What characterizes these events? Hatred, violence, fear, intolerance, prejudice, propaganda, war, persecution, corruption, power struggle, genocide - MINDLESSNESS.

Now turn your attention to the positive events in history. What characterizes them? New inventions, new ideas, innovations, growth, expansion, opportunity and job creation, art and beauty, collaboration, civility, tolerance, security, peace, prosperity, progress, evolution - MINDFULNESS.

To put it simply when Mindfulness is present then thinking is productive and problem solving becomes effective and almost effortless. The lack of mindfulness results in fear, anxiety, quick assumptions, rash decisions, anger, worry and negative and unconsidered actions and consequences. When faced with any problem, centre yourself and then ask yourself "What's the problem here." Your state of mind goes a long way in helping you solve your problems.

"Mindful meditation has been discovered to foster the ability to inhibit those very quick emotional impulses"

- Daniel Goleman

Thinking Defined

OXFORD ENGLISH DICTIONARY DEFINES
THINKING AS FOLLOWS:

- ✓ Exercise the mind in an active way

- ✓ Form connected ideas

- ✓ Form an intention or plan

- ✓ Take things into consideration and consider carefully

- ✓ Call to mind and remember

- ✓ Be of the opinion and judge

- ✓ Try to find a solution to a problem

- ✓ Change one's mind after (re) consideration

- ✓ Invent or produce by thought

- ✓ Using rational judgement about things

*"Thinking is the hardest work there is,
which is probably the reason
why so few engage in it"*

- Henry Ford

So how do you activate your mindfulness? See and practice the items on the following checklist:

✓ Slow down and centre yourself

✓ Close your eyes and take a few slow deep breaths

✓ Clear your mind of pressing negative thoughts

✓ Meditate and use relaxing music if you have it

✓ When centred ask "What's the problem here"

✓ Focus on the things you can do something about

✓ Be objective, keep things in perspective

✓ Open your mind to new ideas and possibilities

✓ Be creative and visualize the possibilities

✓ Use your rationality, logic and reason

✓ Don't use emotion at this stage e.g. DON'T PANIC

✓ Write it down clearly and to the point

✓ Get moving and take action

✓ Review your result and make changes where required

Emotions are important but should not be directing your thinking just fuelling your positive intentions and actions. To be emotionally intelligent is an important ability that helps you to empathise with someone else but should not replace mindfulness. Once mindful you are able to make better and more objective decisions.

Any problem, whether it is related to:

✓ Your house or car

✓ Your career or job

✓ Your relationships

✓ Your education

✓ Your business or finances

✓ Your health

✓ Your mental or emotional well being

requires you to be mindful. You need to regularly review your problems and challenges and see which require attention, maintenance, improvement, or renewal. By not doing this you choose to ignore your problems and hope for the best(!) This is not the mindful approach. Consequences are inescapable, whether neutral, positive or negative. You need to take full responsibility for your problems and deal with them accordingly. This requires you to be mindful of yourself and others, to be present in your life, to take full responsibility for your thinking, emotions, decisions, actions and their consequences and to regularly reflect on your life and make changes where necessary.

*"All that we are is the
result of what
we have thought...
We are formed and
moulded by our thoughts...
The mind is everything,
you become what
you think"*

\- Budda

THEY INTROSPECT ON BELIEFS AND VALUES

"Believe nothing... unless it agrees with reason and common sense"

- Budda

What are beliefs and values and what do they have to do with the quality of effective problem solving? The answer is simple - Everything! Your beliefs and values (especially the ones that you hold dear without questioning) will have a significant impact on the quality of your thinking and problem solving. The quality of your thinking will direct your decisions, actions and the consequences of those actions. Good problem solvers consistently introspect on their beliefs and values. Many people in the world today are stuck in poor actions because their beliefs and values are inadequate.

Some people may consider questioning and challenging current beliefs and belief systems disrespectful, negative and even evil. Positive problem solving has to do with questioning and challenging the status quo and may require changing or adapting your beliefs and values. The good problem solver considers which beliefs and values are harmful and holding her back and works towards changing them for the positive.

People hold onto beliefs and values because of the way they were brought up - tradition, culture, and religion. However, it is historically clear that those people and societies that have not adapted, have had to pay a serious (and in many cases) an unnecessary price. Your beliefs and values can either take you to the stars or keep you in the slums. What you hold onto dearly without questioning, and consider important without introspection, can hold you back from solving many of the problems in your life. So start introspecting if you don't do it already.

"Reason above everything else"

OXFORD ENGLISH DICTIONARY DEFINES BELIEF AND VALUE AS:

Belief Defined

- ✓ The feeling that something is real and true
- ✓ Confidence, trust, something accepted as truth
- ✓ Trust without questioning, evidence, facts or proof

Value Defined

- ✓ Desirability, usefulness and importance
- ✓ The ability of a thing to serve a purpose
- ✓ Something of great worth and importance

The following checklist is a guideline for you to introspect on your current beliefs and values in order for you to improve the quality of your problem solving:

- ✓ Write down your current belief or value clearly?
- ✓ Ask why do you believe or value this?
- ✓ Ask how this belief or value helps you?
- ✓ Ask how this belief or value harms you?
- ✓ Consider if it is positive, negative or neutral?
- ✓ Consider if you should change or adapt it?
- ✓ If you should change then to what?
- ✓ If you don't change what are the consequences?
- ✓ What have you learned from this belief or value so far?
- ✓ What should you keep doing, improve, do different, or stop?
- ✓ What negative attitude should you let go of?
- ✓ What positive attitude should you adopt?
- ✓ Review your beliefs and values regularly

"I would rather have my mind opened by my imagination than closed by a limiting belief"

LOGICAL AND RATIONAL OBJECTIVE AND MORAL AND HAVE GOOD JUDGEMENT

"Face reality as it is, not as it was or as you wish it to be"

- Jack Welch

Problem solving requires you to be conscious of and face reality. You need to be logical and rational, objective and moral and be able to make good judgments. Poor problem solving happens when you lose sight of reality. You need to be able to clearly distinguish facts from opinions. You need to use your mind as the first port of call before intuition and feelings. Poor problem solvers tend to disregard reality and all the facts. They make bad decisions because of poor logic and judgement. Because problem solving also involves interaction with other people, it is important to behave morally and accordingly.

Logic & Rationality Defined

✓ Reasoning correctly and information based on facts

✓ Non contradictory, consistent and in context with reality

✓ Rejecting explanations involving the supernatural

Judgement Defined

✓ The ability to judge wisely

✓ To give an authoritative opinion

✓ To be able to distinguish between and evaluate right and wrong, good and bad, positive and negative

Objectivity Defined

✓ Real existence outside the mind - not subjective

✓ Not influenced by personal feelings and opinions

Morality Defined

✓ Concerned with the good or bad of human character

✓ Principles of what is right and wrong in human conduct

✓ Ethics are a set of principles guiding moral behaviour

Disrespect, inconsideration or just plain negativity are factors that need to be avoided if you are to become a better problem solver. Successful problem solving usually comes down to three things, namely:

✓ The quality of your thinking and information
✓ The quality of your character, people skills and relationships
✓ The availability of quality resources and favourable conditions

By adopting the characteristics of logic, rationality, objectivity, judgement and morality you can be sure to become a better problem solver. Violate these characteristics and you will most certainly fail in your problem solving at one point or another. The key is to become mindful of your thinking and actions. How often do you:

✗ Make bad judgments, lose your temper or panic?
✗ Accept opinions and feelings for facts - ignore reality?
✗ Follow inconsistent and irrational line of thinking?
✗ Treat others poorly and without consideration?
✗ Make quick assumptions and jump to conclusions?

By becoming more mindful you can avoid and prevent such poor behaviours and problems and as a result make better decisions.

"I get the facts,
I study them
patiently,
I apply
imagination"

\- Bernard M. Baruch

THEY ARE CREATIVE AND CAN VISUALIZE

"Imagination is more important than knowledge"

- Albert Einstein

Where would problem solving be without creativity and visualization? Good problem solving requires holistic thinking. This implies thinking that is both critical and creative. Edward de Bono defines creativity as *bringing into being something that was not there before that has value*. Creative thinking is useful when conventional thinking fails to generate solutions to problems. The ability to visualise and create future scenarios is powerful. That is why techniques like mind mapping are so effective. Visualizing involves forming pictures, concepts, feelings and images of solutions.

Visualizing is not always easy for everyone. Some people have trouble seeing in pictures and using their imagination. This is not an issue. Visualization can involve mental pictures, feelings, mind maps and scenarios, so you can use whatever style you prefer. When solving problems you should always write the problem down. Putting pen to paper will make it much easier for you to visualize the problem. When you clarify, write or draw the problem you can use:

✓ Colours, pens, brushes or design software
✓ Pictures, magazines, graphs or drawings
✓ Videos or multimedia

Our minds work with images and using these techniques will make it easier for you to clarify problems and possible solutions. Creativity and visualization go hand in hand. Problem solving would not be the same without these two characteristics. Every problem requires the generating of ideas and by adopting a creative mind set and visualization techniques you can make problem solving much more effective. Remember to let your creativity flow.

CHARACTERISTICS OF CREATIVE PROBLEM SOLVERS:

✓ They can generate many new or better ideas

✓ The can see many ways of doing things not just one way

✓ They can see new and improved ways of doing things

✓ They are original, flexible and able to see things differently

✓ They can connect seemingly unrelated things

✓ They challenge traditional ways of doing things

✓ They can visualize problems and ideas using imagination

✓ They can create new valuable combinations

✓ They are comfortable with making provocations

✓ They ask 'what if' 'why' and 'why not'

✓ They are flexible in their thinking

✓ They delay judgement and keep an open mind

✓ They have a good sense of humour

✓ They can think critically as well as creatively

✓ They can distinguish the big picture from the details

✓ They make experiments and try new things

"Visualize this thing that you want, see it, feel it, believe in it. Make your mental blue print, and begin to build"

- Robert Collier

"Do not go where the path may lead, go instead where there is no path and leave a trail"

\- Ralph Waldo Emerson

THEY ARE CONSIDERATE AND GENUINE

"Courteousness is consideration for others, politeness is the method used to deliver it"

- Bryant H. McGill

C ertainly one of the biggest causes of problems (small or large) worldwide is the lack of consideration. The Oxford English dictionary describes being considerate as *the taking care not to hurt or inconvenience others*. The word consideration is also described in the dictionary as *careful thought, kindness and a fact that must be kept in mind*. Examples of poor consideration can be as large as disrespectful or derogatory behaviour to another based on culture, race, religion, sex or age. Other examples include violating fairness in queues, giving preferential treatment or speaking loudly at the cinema.

Why do people behave in such inconsiderate ways? The answer keeps revealing its ugly head constantly - The active aversion from thinking about the consequences of your actions and how they may affect other people, cultures or environments etc ... Another reason includes the active and conscious pursuit to cause harm to another. Consideration is very similar to Mindfulness. To prevent or solve problems more effectively take note at how your behaviour and actions may affect another or a situation.

The Oxford English dictionary defines genuine as *really what it is said to be, authentic or real.* Good problem solvers exhibit genuine behaviour with other people. They are not fake or hypocritical. People appreciate this quality because it is an indication that you are honest and worthy of trust. Remember to be considerate, polite and genuine with others and you will solve your problems more easily with the help of others.

"People don't care how much you know until they know how much you care"

CHECKLIST TO BE CONSIDERATE

- ✓ Be authentic, real and genuine and really listen

- ✓ Be mindful of your words, actions and behaviours

- ✓ Be mindful of other cultures, languages and traditions

- ✓ Don't discriminate against others superficially

- ✓ Don't be hypocritical or have double standards

- ✓ Make sure you follow the golden rule: treat others as you would like them to treat you - with respect and dignity

- ✓ Use the words: 'Please, Thank you, I am Sorry and Excuse me' more often and show genuine interest and concern

- ✓ Take steps to become more mature - don't actively pursue harming another - as no good can come of active, unprovoked harmful intent

- ✓ Consider for a moment how your actions may be affecting other people and take action to correct them

- ✓ Ask yourself how you would feel if you were in the other persons situation and avoid harming others

"Remember to say Thank You"

THEY ARE NOT SHY
ABOUT ASKING QUESTIONS

"Wisdom begins with Questioning...The most difficult questions to answer are those left unasked, you can't confront ignorance unless you first confront the truth"

Remember when you were a child? You used to be curious about everything. You used to ask questions. You used to get excited about things. Things like ice cream, movies, books, games, outings, friends and playing. The world, as a child, is an exciting and wonderful place. The world was full of mystery and adventure. As a child you just want to know everything about everything there is to know about. You used to ask questions to explore and discover. What happened? Many parents and schools suppress children questioning current beliefs, traditions, ways of doing things or current knowledge.

No wonder that as teenagers and adults we tend to ask much less questions for fear of ridicule, looking stupid in front of others or making mistakes. If you want to improve the quality of your problem-solving you have to be willing to ask all the necessary questions. The more questions you ask about the problem the more likely you will solve the problem. A famous author once wrote that the secret of science is in asking the right question. Get into the habit of asking questions and add the following to your vocabulary:

- ✓ What
- ✓ Why and Why not
- ✓ When
- ✓ Where
- ✓ Who and for Whom
- ✓ How
- ✓ What else
- ✓ What if
- ✓ What next
- ✓ With what
- ✓ How long
- ✓ What for

Write the above questions on a card, laminate it and put it in your wallet or handbag for easy reference. Alternatively, type them on your cell phone, laptop, PC or anywhere else that will be easily accessible to you as reminders. Good problem solvers remember to:

- ✿ Continue asking questions
- ✿ Be sceptical, logical and rational
- ✿ Get and stay informed with credible information
- ✿ Pay close attention and focus
- ✿ Think clearly, critically and creatively
- ✿ Listen clearly
- ✿ Keep an open mind

Every time I am faced with a problem the first thing I do is ask myself, "what is the problem here?" By doing this I am able to mindfully reflect on the problem. These questions activate your rationality. Use them and see your problem solving ability take flight.

"He who asks a question may be a fool for five minutes, but he who never asks a question remains a fool forever"

"*I keep six honest serving men, they taught me all I knew, their names are What and Where and When and How and Why and Who*"

- Rudyard Kipling

THEY TOLERATE MISTAKES, FAILURE AND CONSTANTLY LEARN

"He who never made a mistake never made a discovery"

- Herman Melville

Problem solving is not without making mistakes or failure. Problems that are routine and mistakes that have already been made, certainly do not have to be repeated. However when it comes to solving complex problems you should not shy away from addressing those on the fear that you might fail. Management Consultant Mike Lipkin once said - *FAIL stands for First Action In Learning*. I have always loved the description because it reminds us not to shy away from making mistakes and rather focus on learning from them.

It is important to think clearly and effectively about every problem you face but unforeseen events and consequences can sometimes happen. Don't let that deter you. If you have made a mistake or failed face it, learn from it and move forward quickly. Instead what most poor problem solvers do when they make a mistake or fail is to get stuck on the mistake or failure. They will continue to beat themselves up over it and continue to feel silly and stupid. This is a waste of your good energy and precious time.

Management consultant Tom Peters says the following on this topic *"Fail Forward Fast - no screw ups no learning."* Making mistakes and failing just come with the territory of solving problems. Accept that. Learn from your mistakes and resolve not to repeat the same mistakes and you will become a better problem solver.

> *"The only real mistake*
> *is the one not learned from"*

"Our greatest glory is not in never failing, but in rising up every time we fail"

- Ralph Waldo Emerson

CHECKLIST FOR MISTAKES AND FAILURES:

✓ Acknowledge the reality that you have made a mistake or failed

✓ Identify why you have failed

✓ Learn from history and the mistakes of others

✓ Ask yourself what you can do better or different next time

✓ Record your learning so you will remember next time you review

✓ Keep a lessons log and review and update it regularly so that you don't forget your lessons

✓ Remind yourself that wasting your energy on beating yourself up will not improve the situation

✓ Accept the situation and move on quickly

"Those who do not learn the lessons of history are doomed to repeat them"

THEY EXERCISE SERENITY AND UNDERSTAND ALL THE FORCES

"There is only one way to happiness and that is to cease worrying about things which are beyond the power of our will"

- Epictetus

In all problems we face there are forces that can either assist us or oppose us. The challenge is to understand the forces that are at play in your particular problem and to tap into those forces that would help you solve the problem and neutralize those forces that would stand in your way. By identifying both supportive and oppressive forces you will be in a much more mindful and capable position of assessing of how to go forward. It is also important to understand what forces are within your control to affect or change and what forces are outside of your control.

"Grant me the serenity to accept the things I cannot change, the courage to change the things I can and the wisdom to know the difference"

- Reinhold Niebuhr

The wise thing to do in every problem is to focus your energy on the forces or elements that you have control or influence over and detach from those that are outside of it. Doing this will help you move forward in any problem and avoid all the head and heart ache that comes from trying to control or change things that you really have no power to change.

Yet so much head and heart ache exists because people don't focus on the things they can change but harbour on those things that they really cannot change. This is a very disempowering mentality. Your challenge is to identify the forces for and against you and next to each one indicate whether you have:

✪   Direct control or influence
✪   Indirect control or influence
✪   Outside of your control or influence

In each of the three options stated, it is a good idea to understand the strength of your control or influence. Is your control or influence:

✪   Strong
✪   Medium
✪   Weak or non existent

THEY ARE EMOTIONALLY INTELLIGENT AND INDEPENDENT (Eii)

"The greatest gifts you can give your children are the roots of responsibility and the wings of independence"

- Denis Waitley

Good problem solvers are emotionally intelligent and independent. They are comfortable in their own skin and do not need the emotional approval of someone else to make them feel good or better about themselves. Good problem solvers are confident, responsible, self reliant and exercise choice. That doesn't mean that they are cold, rude, anti-social or don't like the company or attention of others but that they are in control of themselves. They are in control of their own thoughts, emotions and actions. As a result they are considered independent.

These qualities are important for good problem solving because they promote mindfulness and responsibility while discouraging rash emotions like anger, fear, worry and panic. Emotional intelligence and independence keeps the problem solver confident, responsible and self assure. To be emotionally independent you don't close yourself off from people but rather you become more open to yourself. What you think and say about yourself (Out loud and subconsciously) is more important than what others think or say about you.

Great leaders, thinkers and problem solvers that add (and have added) positive value to the world display self control. These individuals understand that their emotions come from their thoughts and so they manage the quality of their thoughts towards positive ends.

"If you are not able to manage your distressing emotions, you are not going to get very far"

- Daniel Goleman

Whenever you feel that your emotions are taking over when your mind should be at work use the phrase HEADS UP either silently to yourself or out loud (if you are in a group) to activate mindfulness. You will see a dramatic difference in your problem solving when your mind is doing the thinking and your heart is doing the feeling and not the other way around.

CHECKLIST TO BE (EII)

✓ Be confident, believe in yourself first and don't be afraid
✓ Get comfortable in your own skin - appreciate yourself
✓ Become more empathetic of yourself and others
✓ Be aware of your thoughts and emotions - learn to control and direct them towards positive ends
✓ Remind yourself that if you are not your own best friend then it becomes harder to be confident, responsible and self reliant because you depend on others and the goal is to become independent and self reliant
✓ Ensure that your SELF esteem comes from yourself FIRST - you have to love yourself before others can love you
✓ Listen to the views and opinions of others but remember that you are ultimately responsible for what you choose to think, feel and act - don't be a victim
✓ Be independent of what others think or say about you

"Nobody can put you on a downer if you don't want to go there, you take full responsibility for yourself and see the difference"

- Leo F. Buscaglia

THEY ARE OPTIMISTIC, INSPIRED AND MOTIVATED

"A man is about as happy as he makes up his mind to be"

- Abraham Lincoln

What is motivation and why is it important in problem solving? The Oxford English Dictionary describes the word motivation as *to give an incentive, stimulate the interest of or inspire*. To solve any problem you should be constantly reminded of the reason, the incentive, the 'Why' or the motivation for solving it. When you solve just about any problem it can either be to acquire more value or pleasure or to reduce or eliminate pain or suffering in life. But whatever the reason for solving your problem, it is so important that you make sure to stay motivated.

Often when you deal with very complicated problems or problems that take more effort or time to address you may become de motivated, uninspired, drained, irritated, annoyed or impatient. These are normal human responses but if you are not aware of your state of thinking or manage it accordingly you may cause more damage to yourself in addressing the problem.

So the challenge of staying motivated is really a challenge of mindfulness, management of your energy and serenity. Many people do not actively manage their motivation and leave it to their mood or the weather. Good problem solvers activate their mindfulness to get motivated. The following checklist highlights some of the things you should consider to stay motivated.

"People often say that motivation doesn't last. Well, neither does bathing, that's why we recommend it daily"

\- Zig Ziglar

STAYING MOTIVATED CHECKLIST:

✓ Keep your goals and success top of mind everyday

✓ Take a break and get back to a state of serenity

✓ Take a clear perspective of the situation

✓ Read an inspiring poem, quote or book

✓ Watch a funny or inspiring movie or video

✓ Play a game and get energized

✓ Listen to inspirational music or talks

✓ Visualize success as clearly as you can - use pictures, videos or photos to connect with your goals

✓ Remind yourself of all the pleasure and success once you accomplish your goal and solve the problem

✓ Remind yourself of all the pain, suffering or frustration that you want to be rid of when you solve the problem

✓ Think of one of your heroes or heroines and ask yourself what keeps (or has kept) them motivated during tough times or when overcoming problems

✓ Believe in yourself first - be confident and remember that people believe in those who truly believe in themselves

✓ Remember to see the glass as half full not half empty

"The pessimist sees difficulty in every opportunity, The optimist sees opportunity in every difficulty"

- Winston Churchill

They have a good sense of humour

"Laughter is the best medicine"

Where would good problem solving be without a good sense of humour? Humour is defined in the Oxford English dictionary as *amusement*. It's important to have a sense of humour because it opens your mind to new ideas, it breaks down tensions between people, and adds positive energy. Good problem solvers are serious about addressing any problem but can still laugh at themselves, the situation, the problem, and the ideas. A good sense of humour is healthy in solving problems because it will ensure that egos and personal tensions dissolve.

Everyone has a sense of humour. Everyone enjoys a good laugh. You don't have to be a clown, stand-up comedian or the president to be funny. What you do need to do is be open to laughing at the situation. Too many people are too serious in the world today. They are angry, anxious, irritated and miserable. Humour uplifts your energy. It makes challenges and problems more bearable. So don't let yourself be miserable. Open your mind, laugh, and see the humour in all things.

CHECKLIST TO BE MORE OPEN TO HUMOUR

✓ Make the effort to smile more often
✓ Try to see the funny side of every problem and situation
✓ Purchase a joke book and read a joke everyday
✓ Laugh with people - don't use humour to harm others
✓ Be willing to laugh at yourself
✓ Remember that humour makes you question
✓ Every time you feel that things are too serious make a joke to break the tension and uplift spirits
✓ A joke adds positive energy and builds relationships
✓ Remember that humour keeps negativity and egos at bay
✓ Humour helps to point out problems and challenge them

"Great minds think alike but fools never differ"

"Don't take life too seriously, after all no one gets out alive"

THEY MANAGE PRIORITIES, TIME AND ARE ORGANIZED

"Do first things First"

- Stephen R. Covey

Good problem solvers manage priorities and time effectively. When addressing any problem they clearly distinguish the important from the urgent. Since you deal with so many problems on a daily basis, it is necessary to distinguish which problems to address first. Poor problem solvers attempt to solve their problems haphazardly. They don't prioritize. They don't manage their time accordingly. As a result they don't solve their problems effectively. The result of poor time and priorities management affects your problem solving.

Mindfulness is essential when managing priorities and time. The world may be spinning out of control around you. You may be stressing about a thousand and one things. But whatever you do, you must make sure that your priorities come first. Simply put, you deal with the more important problems first. You manage your time around your priorities. One of the key skills (and a common theme in this book) is the importance of WRITING your priorities down. When you start your day, WRITE down exactly what you want to accomplish and list your goals in order of importance. Once you have listed what is important and urgent, assign a time when you will begin and when you expect to be finished.

Good problem solvers are organized. They know which goals they need to accomplish, when and in what order of importance. Being organized helps you become more efficient in solving problems. Organized problem solvers have a good filing system and always prepare in advance for challenges ahead. They know when to say NO to people or things by distinguishing between what is urgent and what's important in their lives.

By managing priorities and time you will deal with your problems more effectively and efficiently. You will get the sense that you are in control of your life. As a result you'll gain confidence and a sense that you can trust in yourself to solve just about any problem. The following checklist provides pointers to consider when managing priorities and time:

CHECKLIST FOR PRIORITIES, TIME AND ORGANIZATION:

✓ Write your priorities down in a list, mind map, or diary
✓ Plan your day at the beginning of every day
✓ List exactly what you want to accomplish
✓ Next to each item write if it is urgent, important or both
✓ Write down when you will start and finish each task
✓ Tick off each task you're done with
✓ Know when to say NO to people, things or distractions
✓ Have a filing system - keep it in order and up to date
✓ Don't leave things to the last minute

AS A RULE OF THUMB FOR SETTING PRIORITIES:

✓ Urgent AND Important tasks come first
✓ Important but Not Urgent tasks come second
✓ Urgent but Not Important tasks come third
✓ Not Urgent and Not Important tasks are last or not at all

THEY ARE DISCIPLINED AND PATIENT

"Discipline is the bridge between goals and accomplishment"

- Jim Rohn

Good problem solvers understand that not every problem can be solved overnight. Problem solving requires discipline and patience. Discipline is described in the Oxford English dictionary as *self-control, will-power and restraint.* Patience is described in the Oxford English dictionary as *calm endurance of hardship, inconvenience, delay and perseverance.* Poor problem solvers jump to conclusions, make quick assumptions and do not follow through effectively with plans and actions. The result causes many problems so be mindful.

So how do you become more disciplined and patient? Are these skills that you can suddenly acquire? Unfortunately, the answer for many people is no. The good news is that with practice, these two characteristics can be improved. That is why it is such a good idea to regularly reflect on your problem-solving activities. Use mindfulness to remind yourself to be patient. Not all problems are simple to solve. We have to deal with many uncertainties and problems that stress us. However, it is better to be patient and disciplined in your problem-solving efforts. Use the following checklist in your efforts to enhance these two characteristics:

✓ Don't jump to conclusions or make quick assumptions
✓ Don't lose sight of your priorities
✓ Keep your eyes on solving the problem BUT don't get overwhelmed by the problem itself - take it step by step
✓ Don't have unrealistic expectations
✓ If you fail then get up and try again or try something different - remember that Rome wasn't built in a day
✓ Be patient and persevere in your problem
✓ Keep your cool and detach from negativity
✓ Be confident and emotionally independent

*"It's not that
I'm so smart,
it's just that
I stay with
problems longer"*

- Albert Einstein

THEY CAN BUILD SCENARIOS

"The best way to predict the future is to invent it"

Good problem solvers are able to think ahead. When I was in school, I played on the chess team and even earned gold achievement awards for chess which I think my best friend deserved more than I did. Chess is a game that is often attributed to nerds, and I guess I was one. However, the value that chess teaches you is often understated. It teaches you to think a number of moves ahead in the game as well as in life. The great chess players confirm this in their books. They foresee the moves of the game and predict the moves their opposition will make.

Great chess players use scenarios to predict what can possibly happen next. Once they visualize the different scenarios they attempt to lead the other player into those scenarios. To start building scenarios use the following guidelines:

✓ Slow down! Don't just move for the sake of moving
✓ Be objective, have patience and think clearly
✓ Understand the rules of the game you are in
✓ Understand the problem and challenge clearly
✓ Understand the interests of all stakeholders
✓ Understand your own strengths and weaknesses
✓ Understand all the forces and limitations at play
✓ Think a number of moves ahead and attempt to lead the game instead of just playing from move to move
✓ Ask 'what if' and consider the consequences
✓ Consider how the environment or rules may change
✓ Make objective speculations and calculations
✓ Use visualization techniques to picture future scenarios
✓ Learn from others, past mistakes and history's lessons
✓ Consider the different perspectives and consequences

Problem solving requires you to be proactive and you can do this by getting better at building scenarios.

Using scenario thinking you may say that if event X happens then the result will be consequence Y and your response can be decision Z. However if event A happens the result will be consequence B and your response can be decision C. For each given scenario, consider how likely it is to occur. Is it:

- ✪ Severely unlikely
- ✪ Not likely
- ✪ Uncertain
- ✪ Likely
- ✪ Very likely

Is the likelihood based on your intuition or trends, facts or opinions, is it plausible and feasible, is it possible given the current realities, technologies, cultures, systems and limitations?

"Are you a creature of circumstance or a creator of circumstance"

THEY HAVE COURAGE
AND CONFIDENCE

"Courage is resistance to fear, mastery of fear, not absence of fear"

- Mark Twain

Good problem solvers are confident. The Oxford English dictionary describes confidence as *a feeling of certainty and self-reliance*. Good problem solvers are assertive and self-assured. They believe in themselves and have a strong sense of self-worth. To be confident doesn't mean that you have to step on or harm other people. It means that you truly trust in yourself, in your skills, abilities and the value that you add. Many problems are intimidating. You have to be able to believe in yourself. Courage is defined as *the ability to face danger without fear*.

Many people fail at problem solving, not because they don't have the skills or abilities but that they lack the confidence and courage. Yes, the problems in your life are challenging. But if you don't believe in yourself and face your fears you will not achieve your full potential or solve your problems. Good problem solvers affirm their value and self-worth to themselves. They realise that even if they make mistakes and fail, they must continue to persevere. There is an old saying that goes 'if I am not for myself then who will be for me'. Good problem solvers believe in themselves first.

CHECKLIST FOR CONFIDENCE AND COURAGE

- ✿ Stand up for and believe in yourself - Don't be afraid
- ✿ Use affirmation and reflection to assert yourself
- ✿ Remember that old proverb that if you don't believe in yourself others will not believe in you
- ✿ Remember that problems will always exist and it is better to have confidence and courage when facing them
- ✿ Remember that confidence starts with your SELF
- ✿ Remember that old lyric that 'learning to LOVE yourself is the greatest love of all' - this is the root of confidence
- ✿ Remember that FEAR can only be overcome with courage

"I must not fear.
Fear is the mind-killer.
I will face my fear.
I will permit it to pass
over me and through me...
and when it has gone...
there will be nothing.
Only I will remain"

\- Frank Herbert

THEY ARE RESPONSIBLE, TRUSTWORTHY, HAVE INTEGRITY AND CHOOSE

"The highest possible stage in moral culture is when we recognize that we ought to control our thoughts"

- Charles Darwin

G ood problem solvers are responsible individuals. They take full responsibility for their beliefs, values, thoughts, feelings, decisions, actions and the consequences of those actions. They exercise choice proactively. They understand that by becoming responsible and proactively choosing they take control of their lives. Good problem solvers are trustworthy and have integrity. This means that you can be relied upon and that you are honest and incorruptible. When you adopt these qualities you can be sure to become a better problem solver.

Responsible Defined

✓ Legally or morally obliged to take care of something

✓ Having to account for one's actions

✓ Capable of rational conduct

Trustworthy Defined

✓ Firm belief in the reliability, truth or strength of something

✓ Worthy of trust and reliable person or thing

Integrity Defined

✓ Honesty, incorruptibility, wholeness and soundness

Choice Defined

✓ A variety from which to choose

✓ Select out of a greater number of things

✓ Decide, prefer, or desire

All these qualities have one thing in common. In order to be a successful problem solver you have to become mindful of your choices. You have to take full responsibility for your thoughts, decisions and actions. You have to use your good judgement to make positive decisions and take positive action.

Good problem solvers have integrity. They display good character. They are honest with themselves and with others. Integrity, trustworthiness, responsibility and the ability to proactively choose are characteristics that work together to make you a better problem solver. If you think about it so many of the problems that we experience in the world today are the result of:

- ✗ Dishonesty, lying and lack of trust
- ✗ People not taking responsibility for their actions
- ✗ People making bad decisions and choices
- ✗ Corruption and lack of morality and integrity
- ✗ Lack of respect and consideration for self and others
- ✗ Having double standards and being unfair

"Whatever is begun in anger ends in shame"

- Benjamin Franklin

"Between stimulus and response is a space, in that space lies your freedom to choose your response, in those choices lie your growth and happiness"

\- Stephen R. Covey

THEY CAN CHANGE
AND ADAPT QUICKLY

*"Anything can be changed if you
dedicate yourself to the process"*

- Leo F. Buscaglia

Problems and challenges are not always static. They can change, evolve and morph. Good problem solvers understand that if things don't work out as planned or if the circumstances change, so too must they. Poor problem solvers get scared of changing. They think that if they ignore the change around them, that it will not affect them. This is clearly a mindless approach as change and its consequences will catch up to you at one point or another. Good problem solvers seek to understand the change clearly and then take action to solve the problem.

It is your inability to recognize that you need to change or adapt that keeps you from solving the problems in your life. Management consultant Tom Peters once said that, "it only takes a second to attain change but a lifetime to maintain it." You must realise that change may not be easy but it is necessary if you are to get unstuck from your present pattern (of thinking or action) and move into a new one. Effective problem solving cannot take place if you are not willing to change your approach or be open to try different ones altogether.

CHECKLIST TO BECOME BETTER AT CHANGE:

- ✓ Activate your mindfulness
- ✓ Ask yourself "What or who needs to change here?"
- ✓ Consider if the change is inside or outside of you
- ✓ Be reasonable and objective - Don't Panic!
- ✓ Consider all the factors that will need to change
- ✓ Consider all the stakeholders to involve
- ✓ Where are you now in relation to where you want to be
- ✓ Consider all the consequences related to the change
- ✓ Visualize and portray the change clearly
- ✓ Define success "the change will be a success when..."
- ✓ Source all the knowledge and resources required
- ✓ Write it all down in a action plan
- ✓ Take action, monitor regularly and learn

"It is not the strongest of the species that survives, nor the most intelligent that survives. It is the one that is the most adaptable to change"

\- Charles Darwin

THEY COMMUNICATE CLEARLY AND LISTEN

"Why need I volumes, if one word would suffice"

- Ralph Waldo Emerson

S ome of the biggest causes of problems in the world are because people don't communicate clearly or effectively with one another. Sometimes problems are caused because people make assumptions and jump to conclusions based on what they 'think' they heard. Sometimes problems are the result of over complicating communication. Poor problem solvers are bad listeners. They tend to talk far more than listen. They may give the impression that they are listening but all they are interested in is in having their say without hearing feedback.

Poor problem solvers complicate their communications. The reasons for complicating rather than simplifying communications comes from our schooling as well as our want to show off 'how clever we are' (Ego). Good problem solvers do just the opposite. They understand the importance of listening carefully without jumping to conclusions or making quick assumptions. They also understand that simplifying a message is better for clearer communication as long as the message is not lost. Good problem solvers are open to communicating with others. They invite others to give feedback and genuinely listen to what is said. Remember that in order to solve any problem (especially with the help of others) you have got to be able to communicate your message clearly and be able to listen to others effectively without jumping to conclusions or making quick assumptions.

✓ Communicate simply and avoid jargon
✓ Check that the message is clear and easy to understand
✓ Be open to feedback and encourage suggestions
✓ Listen Listen Listen - don't just assume you know
✓ Check that you understand and that you are understood
✓ Don't be rude or interrupt others - let them have their say
✓ Say what you mean and mean what you say

"Listen, or thy tongue will keep thee deaf"

- American Indian Proverb

THEY CAN OVERCOME NEGATIVITY AND DETACH

"Those who are free of resentful thoughts surely find peace"

- Budda

G ood problem solvers know how to manage their own negativity as well as detach from the negativity of others. In solving just about any problem you will encounter some negative people and situations. The good problem solver doesn't let the negativity of others or the situation affect her goal. Poor problem solvers tend to get caught up in a web of emotional blackmail, negativity and as a result, don't effectively solve their problems. But how do you guard yourself against the negative energy of other people? How do you detach from negativity?

First and foremost you need to activate your mindfulness and realise that adopting a negative attitude (as discussed earlier) will not help you solve the problem better. You need to stop feeling sorry for yourself and get out of the rut you may have dug for yourself. Most importantly, you need to let go of your anger. Remember that any emotion (positive or negative) is the result of your thoughts which you can choose. So be mindful and choose thoughts that will lead to positive emotions.

HOW TO OVERCOME NEGATIVITY

✓ Recognize and acknowledge that you are negative
✓ Centre, take slow deep breaths, calm down and relax
✓ Go somewhere else to cool off, and reflect
✓ Use humour to jump start positive energy or to jolt yourself out of a negative state of mind
✓ Decide that you would rather be positive and objective than negative and emotional in addressing the problem
✓ Write down what you are negative about - be specific
✓ What is causing the negativity - what can be done?
✓ Consider and list the options - use creativity and reason
✓ Consider the consequences of your actions and be mindful - do you prefer to experience the positive or negative consequences of your actions?
✓ Take responsibility and action
✓ Don't be a victim

"Holding on to anger is like grasping a hot coal with the intent of throwing it at someone else; you are still the one getting burned"

- Budda

THEY SHOW EMPATHY
AND FORGIVENESS

*"Forgiveness saves the expense of anger, the
cost of hatred and the waste of spirits"*

- Hannah More

Good problem solvers understand the value of empathy
and forgiveness. Empathy is defined in the dictionary as
*caring, compassion, sensitivity, sympathy and under-
standing*. Good problem solvers understand that when
working with other people it is important to show
empathy. Working with machines, computers and things
obviously doesn't require empathy. Things don't have
emotions or feelings and cannot be upset or de motivated.
People can and do. Good problem solvers can put themselves in the other persons shoes and be empathetic.

Forgiveness is described in the dictionary as *amnesty, excusing, overlooking, pardoning and releasing*. In order to forgive somebody you decide to let go of the past transgressions. Poor problem solvers have difficulty showing forgiveness. In other words, they have difficulty letting go of the past. They remain angry and bitter. Good problem solvers understand that by forgiving the past or another person, they release themselves from the past negativity, pain, hurt or sadness. Good problem solvers do not forget the past, instead they detach and learn from it. Poor problem solvers don't learn the lessons of the past and history, instead they repeat the very same mistakes of poor problem solvers that came before them. Forgiveness doesn't require the other person to be present, just your own mindfulness and the decision to let go of the past negativity that is keeping you upset. Some problems can be avoided and solved just by becoming more empathetic with other people and being able to forgive others as well as yourself.

"Heal the Past, Live the Present, Dream the Future"

"Acceptance of what has happened is the first step to overcoming the consequences of any misfortune"

- William James

THEY CAN NEGOTIATE EFFECTIVELY

*"Don't negotiate out of fear but
don't ever fear to negotiate"*

- John F. Kennedy

G ood problem solvers are effective negotiators. Poor problem solvers have the "it's my way or the highway" attitude. They are not willing to listen to others or to understand the others point of view. Negotiation is defined in the dictionary as *discuss in order to reach an agreement* or *succeed in passing round or over a problem*. Negotiation requires you to be mindful and considerate of the other person and to listen clearly. Good problem solvers understand that when dealing with just about any problem, people may not always agree.

This is where negotiation comes in. To improve your negotiation skills you have to park your ego and prejudice at the door. You need to be willing to see the other persons perspective. You need to use your objectivity, rationality and logic to understand the problem, and then to use your creativity to think of alternatives that will satisfy all the people in the negotiation. Use the phrase 'What will make you happy OR What will satisfy your needs' when negotiating. Get all parties to list their requirements, needs and definition of success and identify ways to reach an agreement. If you really cannot come to an agreement that would satisfy all the people then everyone should agree to disagree agreeably.

CHECKLIST FOR NEGOTIATION

✓ Decide to be mature, rational and creative

✓ Listen to the others point of view and keep an open mind

✓ Write everything down clearly and to the point

✓ Consider how you can satisfy everyone's requirements

✓ Use the SCAMPER technique to generate ideas

✓ If you cannot agree then agree to disagree agreeably

"A problem well defined is a problem half solved"

\- Albert Einstein

HEADS UP!
THERE'S A PROBLEM

"Open your eyes, open your mind...an open mind is far more powerful than a clenched fist"

Problems are better addressed when they are clearly defined and understood. Poor problem solvers make quick assumptions and jump to finding solutions before they have defined or clarified what the problem actually is in the first place. In dealing with (just about) any problem your challenge is to become mindful of yourself and the world around you. Many people suffer with problems because they don't know how to recognize, clarify and face their problems effectively and as a result they feel anxious and overwhelmed most of the time.

Your challenge is to define clearly what the problems are in your particular situation. Is the problem 'out there' or 'within you'? Is the problem within your control or outside of your control? Do you clearly understand what the problem is? Can you summarize it into a concise sentence? Are you being proactive or reactive? Are you dealing with part of the problem or the total problem? Are you taking full responsibility for addressing the problem or are you avoiding and ignoring it? Are you objective and reasonable or out of control and emotional?

A great phrase I like to use to activate a mindful state is "HEADS UP". Like the Ostrich, poor problem solvers stick their heads in the ground, panic, get anxious, reactive and as result solve their problems poorly or not at all. Good problem solvers activate their mindfulness. They take responsibility, use objectivity, logic, creativity and choose to be positive and proactive in addressing the problem at hand.

"Begin with Reason, follow through with Passion"

CLARIFY, LABEL AND DEFINE THE PROBLEM

"Make everything as simple as possible, but not simpler"

- Albert Einstein

One of the biggest causes of poor problem solving comes down to not clarifying or labelling problems correctly. Poor problem solvers tend to misdiagnose or mislabel their problems and as a result, solve their problems ineffectively or not at all. As discussed earlier, good problem solvers activate their mindfulness. Once they are mindful they ask themselves the question "what is the problem here?" Once this question is asked you need to clarify specifically the problem at hand and then label it as clearly and specifically as possible.

The purpose of labelling a problem is to clarify what the problem is. You might say "this is a medical problem or that is a marketing problem." The label makes clarifying and defining the problem much easier. It is also useful to elaborate on the label by using a descriptive adjective. For example, you might say "this is a *routine* medical problem or that is a *complex* finance problem or this is a *simple* relationship problem." Once the problem is clarified use the phrase TO DO WITH to elaborate further on the problem label. For example "this is a marketing problem TO DO WITH promoting products to customers during the December holidays." The key is to be as specific as possible. If many people are addressing the same problem you must ensure that they all understand and agree with the problem statement.

Consider if the problem is routine, unique or combination of both? By answering these questions and labelling the problem the generating of ideas becomes far more effective. The solutions for a routine problem would come from existing information, knowledge, and research as well as from experts who have addressed this problem (or a similar one) before.

If someone has already solved the problem you are facing it is more efficient to learn from that person than re-invent the wheel unnecessarily. The solutions for a unique problem require creative efforts and techniques such as lateral thinking, visualization, experiments, prototypes, brainstorming and mind mapping to name just a few.

If the problem is a combination of both routine and unique, it is important to recognise which aspect of the problem is which. Those aspects that are routine can be solved using existing knowledge and those that are unique can be solved creatively. One of the key skills of becoming a better problem solver is to be able to see a situation from many different perspectives. Good problem solvers can see the problem from one perspective and then shift their perspective to see the problem from a different one.

"Who is Wise?
One who learns from every man"
- Zoma

The key skill is to listen and to keep an open mind. A closed or arrogant mind will refuse to see the different perspectives of a problem. The closed mind will refuse to acknowledge that 'it' may be part of the problem. That is why it is important to park your ego at the door. For a problem to be well defined you need to be able and willing to see all the angles and all the perspectives concerning it.

CHECKLIST FOR LABELING PROBLEMS MORE EFFECTIVELY

- ✓ Is it simple or complicated?
- ✓ Is it routine, unique or a combination of both?
- ✓ Is it general or specific?
- ✓ Is it out there or within you?
- ✓ Is it a symptom or a cause?
- ✓ In how many other ways can you define the problem?
- ✓ Are you looking at the problem from all perspectives?
- ✓ What need or want is the problem related to?
- ✓ Do all stakeholders agree with the problem statement?
- ✓ Are you listening clearly?
- ✓ Are you objective and fair?
- ✓ Can you see the forest from the trees?
- ✓ Consider what you may be missing

"Sometimes the situation is only a problem because it is looked at in a certain way. Looked at in another way, the right course of action may be so obvious that the problem no longer exists"

- Edward de Bono

WRITE IT DOWN AND KISS IT!

"Our life is frittered away by details ... Simplify Simplify"

- Henry David Thoreau

Problem solving is easy when it is clear what the problem is in the first place. Poor problem solving happens when the problem is not clarified or understood. When you face any problem you should write it down as clearly and concisely as possible. Writing down a problem and keeping it simple helps with the clarification of it. Poor problem solvers jump to conclusions and start looking for solutions before they clearly understand the problem. If the problem is written down, clarified, discussed and simplified, then the real problem begins to emerge.

KISS stands for KEEP IT SHORT AND SIMPLE. Whatever problem you face, no matter what it is, if you have a clear statement and an understanding of it, you will be in a much better and more effective position to address it. Just think, whether the problem is in business, in a relationship or a personal situation, you will be in a much better position to solve the problem if:

✓ You are mindful, objective, logical and reasonable
✓ You clearly understand the problem
✓ Your stakeholders understand the problem
✓ The problem is written down and visible
✓ The problem is described clearly and concisely

Yet, when you observe poor problem solvers, you will find the opposite characteristics from the above list. Poor problem solvers lose their cool and jump to conclusions. They don't clearly understand the problem and are not on the same page with their stakeholders or partners in the understanding of the problem. The problem is not written down. The problem is often confusing and not clearly understood. So remember to KISS so you can kiss your problems goodbye.

DEFINE THE CRITICAL SUCCESS FACTORS

"The limited number of areas in which results, if they are satisfactory, will ensure success"

- John F. Rockart

Critical success factors are the elements in your problem that you want to accomplish, achieve, or acquire. When you successfully solve your problem, each and every one of your critical success factors is addressed. So what is the definition of success in your current problem? Good problem solvers define their critical success factors clearly. Critical success factors can be used to measure to what degree you have solved your problem. Poor problem solvers don't define their critical success factors clearly and accomplish mediocre results.

After a problem is clearly defined the next question to ask is "what does success look like?" An example phrase I like to use and answer is "I will be successful or overcome the problem when..." and then list and elaborate on each element clearly. To define your critical success factors simply write a list of all the factors or elements that need to be addressed in your problem solving effort. Then elaborate on how each element contributes to the success of your problem. Define by which date should success be accomplished. Define to what quality or standard should each factor adhere to. Critical success factors can be presented in various ways including: lists, diagrams, percentages, presentations, share prices, drawings, schematics, and formulas.

CHECKLIST FOR CRITICAL SUCCESS FACTORS

✓ List and elaborate on your definition of success
✓ Be as specific as possible
✓ Finish the following sentence "I will succeed / overcome the problem when..."
✓ Consider the quality standard you want to accomplish
✓ Consider the deadline that you want to be finished by
✓ Ensure that goals and critical success factors align

Ask an Expert or Qualified Professional

*"If I have seen further than others,
it is by standing upon the shoulders of giants"*

- Sir Isaac Newton

M any problems you face on a daily basis don't have to be addressed on your own. There are so many experts and specialists in the world that make a living to help others solve their problems. Whenever you are faced with a problem that you are uncertain about, the first thing you should do is to find an expert in that field that can advise you and help you to solve the problem. It is silly and arrogant not to take advantage of the vast expertise that is available in the world today. There is simply no excuse, we are living in a world that is an ocean of information.

Access to expertise is abundant. Don't be lazy or arrogant. Experts can teach you about their area of expertise and experience. What has worked in the past and what has not. The Internet is brilliant for finding and accessing experts around the world and for finding answers to questions. Use mediums such as search engines, online forums, blogs, chat rooms, encyclopedias, books, (electronic) journals, articles, podcasts, google.com, wikipedia.org, answers.com, ehow.com and howstuffworks.com to name just a few.

However, make sure that the expert or specialist providing information is accredited to do so. As a problem solver you can't just go on opinion or faith. You have to ensure that your thinking is directed by facts, objectivity, logic and good judgement. Don't just take the word, general opinion or views of those who (even if they are your family or friends and have your best interests at heart) don't have all the necessary information, expertise or qualification to solve the problem.

"When the student is ready the teacher will appear"

RESEARCH AND
GATHER INFORMATION

> *"He who does not increase*
> *his knowledge decreases it"*
>
> - Hillel

The good problem solver does her research. It is important to gather as much information as possible about the problem in order to decide how to go forward in your problem solving effort. Poor problem solvers ONLY use their intuition and gut feel. It is certainly important to acknowledge and use your intuition in solving problems. However, you should never replace research and the gathering of information with intuition and gut feel. Research is objective (based on facts) and intuition is subjective (based on belief, feeling or opinion).

RESEARCH IS USEFUL IN:

✓ Discovering how others face the same or similar problem
✓ Testing how people or things respond to the problem
✓ Understanding the facts surrounding the problem
✓ Testing your hypotheses using scientific methods
✓ Learning from the problem and advancing for the future

It is important to be objective and scientific in your research approach. Use journals, books, white papers, encyclopedias, online sources, interviews, surveys, polls and questionnaires to gather information. The information that you gather needs to be up to date, credible and reliable. Use the information standards checklist in the following chapter to assess the validity of any information that you use in solving your problems. Remember to always distinguish between:

✓ What information you have (and know for a fact)
✓ What information you still need (or need to verify)

"He who has the most information will have the greatest success in life"
- Disraeli

THE INFORMATION STANDARDS CHECKLIST

"True genius resides in the capacity for evaluation of uncertain, and conflicting information"

- Winston Churchill

Problem solving requires you to be objective, rational, reasonable and creative. However if you don't have all (or as much as necessary or possible) of the information available it will be difficult to address or solve anything. Often, the causes of problems result from not having all or enough of the information available. What is worse is that we tend to try solve the problem with little or speculative information which leads to even more problems. We lose our temper, make assumptions, jump to conclusions and make unsupported pre-judgements.

You can run into many problems and frustrations if you are trying to solve a problem that you don't have enough information for or not fully understand. So what is the message here? Make sure you have all the necessary information at hand before you attempt to solve the problem. Einstein once said, "If I had a problem upon which my life depended and I only had one hour in which to solve it, I would spend 40 minutes to gather information, 15 minutes to review information and 5 minutes to develop solutions."

The lesson is this, when addressing any problem take more time to understand the problem and then proceed to take action - currently the reverse is true with most people and organizations. You have to be objective and see all perspectives of the problem. You have to be honest with yourself and others. Use the information standards checklist on the following page to assess the information available to solve just about any problem.

> *"If you have ten seconds to make a decision, think for nine"*
>
> - Jeffery J. Fox

USE THIS CHECKLIST TO ASSESS ANY INFORMATION, IS IT...

- ✓ Accurate and precise?
- ✓ Appropriate and applicable?
- ✓ Based on evidence and objective reality?
- ✓ Clear and specific?
- ✓ Comparing apples with apples?
- ✓ Complete in terms of depth and breadth?
- ✓ Representative or sufficient to make a decision?
- ✓ Consistent and repeatable?
- ✓ Credible, referenced, verifiable and trustworthy?
- ✓ Current and up to date?
- ✓ Facts distinguished from opinions or anecdotes?
- ✓ Fair and without prejudice?
- ✓ Logical, objective, valid and without logical fallacy?
- ✓ Non contradictory or misleading?
- ✓ Provided by an accredited and qualified person?
- ✓ Providing evidence or proof?
- ✓ Rational, reasonable and without ego?
- ✓ Relevant to the situation?
- ✓ Reliable person or sources?
- ✓ Reproducible under the same circumstances?
- ✓ Reputable or a recommended source?
- ✓ Scientific and measurable?
- ✓ Undistorted and unbiased?

"What can be asserted without evidence, can also be dismissed without evidence"

- Christopher Hitchens

CLARIFY REQUIREMENTS AND CONCERNS OF ALL STAKEHOLDERS

"You're never quite as stupid as when you think you already know everything"

Some problems can be solved on your own but there are many problems that require dealing and working with other people. When you deal with other people to solve the same problem some challenges arise. The most important challenge is to ensure that everyone agrees on the definition of the overall problem. This is called *being on the same page* with other people. You will find that many problems exist in groups because people do not understand, agree with or care how others see the problem. Problems in groups cannot be solved this way.

The challenge is to get groups to come together, voice and come to an agreement on what:

✓ The problem is ... (Be specific)
✓ The problem is not ... (Highlight the boundaries)

This is also known as clarifying the scope of the problem. By acknowledging the importance of other people and getting them to communicate what they:

✓ See the problem to be - their views and concerns
✓ Want to get from the solution - their requirements

You will be able to (with their support) solve the problem better. Poor problem solving happens when many people who don't agree on the scope of the problem try to solve the problem together. The result is chaos. So in the next problem you address with other people make sure to:

✓ WRITE DOWN and include their views
✓ Understand what their requirements are
✓ Listen carefully and objectively and
✓ Acknowledge their importance in the process

People who are not on the same page will not solve the problem effectively or at all.

CLARIFY ALL ASSUMPTIONS, CONSIDERATIONS AND CONSEQUENCES

"Most of our assumptions have outlived their usefulness"

Poor problem solving happens when you don't consider all the factors that need to be considered. When you make quick assumptions without checking the facts and when you don't consider all the consequences of your ideas, beliefs, values, decisions and actions. Good problem solving happens when you consider all the factors that need to be considered to address the problem. This requires mindfulness. Also, explore what happens when you drop all your assumptions individually or in combination to see how many new insights you can get.

The A - Z Considerations List in part 8 of this book is a good starting point to prompt your thinking on what should be considered when attempting to solve your problems. Consequences (especially in the longer term) are often ignored. The good problem solver considers all the consequences of her actions (both short and long term) and makes better decisions to suit. Refer to the Consequences Template in part 8 of the book to help you make better decisions for the longer term.

CHECKLIST TO CONSIDER

✓ List all the things that need to be considered

✓ If you are dealing with other people get their views

✓ List and challenge all the assumptions

✓ List all the possible consequences over time

✓ Think clearly and keep the problem as the focus

✓ Be realistic, objective and reasonable

✓ Don't get side tracked

"It is never too late to give up our prejudices"

\- Henry David Thoreau

HAVE A DICTIONARY
OR ENCYCLOPEDIA READY

"Always be Prepared"

- The Boy Scouts

One of the major causes of problems is when you address a problem but get stuck because you don't understand the definition, meaning or background history. I titled this segment 'Have a Dictionary or Encyclopedia ready' because that is exactly what you should have on hand if you do get stuck to understand a problem and need a credible definition or source. In the business world, in schools, universities, as well in politics, poor problem solvers pretend to know what's going on to look clever and to impress their bosses or peers.

One common thing that happens is, that when faced with a concept or situation that is not understood, poor problem solvers will not ask questions and will keep quiet for fear of looking silly and being ridiculed. It is better to ask questions to understand and verify your understanding than be left behind in the dark and hope you will understand the problem later. If you really don't have the opportunity to ask at that particular moment make sure you make a note to ask or look up the definition as soon as possible.

If there is a misunderstanding when it comes to defining a term then simply turn to a credible definition of the term or concept using a dictionary, encyclopedia or reliable (objective) information source. This eliminates arguments and misunderstandings based on opinion. In a world of virtually free and abundant information, there is no excuse to be left in the dark regarding understanding definitions, concepts and critical information.

NOTE:

✓ Prepare a dictionary, encyclopedia, map and the tools

Consider your SWOT

"He who knows when he can and cannot fight,
will be victorious ... If ignorant both of your enemy
and yourself, you are certain to be in peril"

- Sun Tzu

Taking note of these four attributes can be powerful in the problem solving process. Before you begin any problem solving effort, consider your SWOT:

✓ STRENGTHS (Yours and your competitors)
✓ WEAKNESSES (Yours and your competitors)
✓ OPPORTUNITIES (Sources of value and benefit)
✓ THREATS (Sources of difficulty or danger)

A strength is defined in the dictionary as *a quality or ability considered to be an advantage*. A weakness is the opposite of a strength and thus a disadvantage.

Recognizing a weakness is the first step in overcoming it. Good problem solvers know where their strengths and weaknesses lie through consistent reflection. Poor problem solvers do not reflect on their strengths or weaknesses. Opportunities are defined as *favorable conditions or events*. Good problem solvers use their mindfulness, objectivity and creativity to spot opportunities and to act on them. Threats are dangers that you should take into consideration when solving your problem. By reflecting on these four questions and applying them to your problem you will get a far better idea of where you stand in the context of the problem.

CHECKLIST FOR SWOT

✓ Write down and compare strengths - advantages and the things done well - be objective not arrogant

✓ Write down and compare weaknesses - things done poorly, things that are unpleasant and can be avoided

✓ Consider the opportunities in (TESPGLM) - technology, economics, society, politics, globally, legal and markets

✓ Consider the obstacles you face, how could the changes in (TESPGLM) threaten you?

✓ Consider forces for and against you and their strengths

BE LIKE A CHILD
ASK: WHY WHY WHY...

"No problem can sustain the
assault of good thinking"

Problems can only be addressed when you begin to understand their real causes. Good problem solvers seek to understand the causes of their problems clearly. A cause is described in the dictionary as *something that produces a particular result or effect*. The best way to understand the cause of a problem is to ask WHY. This wonderful word is defined in the dictionary as *for what reason* and it is precisely the tool that you should use to understand the causes and the reasons behind the problems that you are facing.

Remember to continue to ask WHY. Children are famous for this behaviour. They continue to ask why, why and why. This may seem irritating to grown-ups but by employing this technique they uncover the causes and the reasons for the way things are. Good problem solvers use this technique to get to the roots of problems quickly. For the problem you are currently facing all you have to do is to continue to ask 'Why why why...' or 'What is the reason for...' until you reach the root cause.

CHECKLIST FOR WHY WHY WHY...

✓ Be like a child and ask 'why why why...'
✓ Ask why a problem is occurring and then continue asking why numerous more times to identify the true underlying cause
✓ Be objective, reasonable and honest with yourself
✓ Write it all down as it will be easier to analyze the cause
✓ Don't be embarrassed to ask questions

"The important thing is not to stop questioning"

- Albert Einstein

CONSIDER ALL ANGLES
OF THE CAUSES

"Shallow men believe in luck,
Strong men believe in cause and effect"

- Ralph Waldo Emerson

To solve problems better you need to clearly understand the causes of your problems. When dealing with and attempting to solve complicated problems, one of the main challenges will be to identify all the causes. Simple problems tend to have fewer causes and can be solved relatively routinely. Complicated problems have far more causes and will require more thinking to identify them. In conjunction with the 'Why why why...' Technique discussed in the previous section it is also important to look at the different angles of the causes.

What this practically means is that you consider all the different angles and list all the factors that could contribute to the cause of the problem. The 'Why why why...' technique is useful in uncovering some of the factors that cause the problem. However, by investigating other areas you will broaden your perspective and be better equipped to address the problem. For example; consider and list all factors and angles that are contributing causes to your problem. Make sure you speak to other people to ensure you see all the perspectives. Then under each cause ask 'why why why...' until you reach the root reason. Be mindful and patient and dedicate specific time just to investigate causes.

CHECKLIST FOR ANGLES OF CAUSES

✓ Consider all the factors and angles of the causes

✓ Keep an open mind and investigate the causes until you get to the root of the problem

✓ Be patient and mindful when looking for causes

✓ Use this approach in conjunction with the 'Why why why...' technique

✓ Make sure you have dedicated time to investigate just the causes without jumping to solutions

VERIFY THE CAUSES

"Reason and free inquiry are the only effectual agents against error"

- Thomas Jefferson

O ne of the most important challenges in the problem solving process is to clearly identify the root causes. As mentioned previously, poor problem solvers make quick assumptions and jump to conclusions when it comes down to addressing problems. The mindful approach is to think objectively about the causes of the problem and ensure you understand them. Once you have considered all the factors, listed all the possible causes and looked at the causes from all the different angles and perspectives you need to verify.

Verify is defined in the dictionary as *check the truth or accuracy of.* All the causes identified need to be verified. It is no good coming up with ideas to address the wrong cause of the problem. Use the *information standards checklist* as a guideline to verify all the factors, angles, perspectives and causes of your problem. Before you begin to generate ideas you must be sure that you understand the causes of the problem so that your creative efforts will be directed effectively.

CHECKLIST TO VERIFY CAUSES

✓ Be objective and honest with yourself and others
✓ Use the information standards checklist to verify
✓ Be sure to clearly understand the problem and its causes before you begin to generate ideas
✓ Make sure that all stakeholders also agree with you

The next section of the book examines some powerful tools and techniques to enhance your creativity in order to address and solve your problems better.

"Measure Twice, Cut Once"

"The problems of the world cannot possibly be solved by sceptics or cynics whose horizons are limited by the obvious realities. We need men who can dream of things that never were"

- John F. Kennedy

THE CREATIVE CHEF RULES!

*"An essential aspect of creativity
is not being afraid to fail"*

- Edwin Land

Ayn Rand defines creation as *to bring into existence an arrangement (combination or integration) of natural elements that had not existed before*. Creative thinking is useful when conventional thinking fails in finding solutions to unique problems. The following sections practically elaborate on creativity techniques to help you come up with ideas that would not have come up traditionally. One of my favourite analogies for creativity is that it's like being a chef in a kitchen - experimenting with different combinations and designing new recipes.

"The winner is the chef who takes the same ingredients as everyone else and produces the best results"

- Edward De Bono

As a chef you have at your disposal:

✿ Many different Ingredients, spices and sauces
✿ Past recipes and current recipes
✿ Pots and pans and other cooking materials
✿ Materials to decorate your creation

How do chefs come up with new recipes? They consider what it is they want to create and who their audience is. They consider the ingredients and materials at hand. They experiment with new and different taste combinations. They chop and change ingredients - mixing and matching methods, tastes, colours, textures and smells until something valuable emerges. They test their recipe and get feedback from their audience and refine the recipe where necessary. Once they are satisfied, they write it up in a recipe book (available for others to copy and use). Similarly, if you want to be more creative learn the lesson of the chef - experiment, be willing to try new things and fail, mix and match different combinations and use your senses. The following sections elaborate on the subject of creativity and the practical aspects of becoming more creative using specific techniques.

'Rules' for Creativity

✓ Make substitutions

✓ Create new combinations

✓ Create new relationships between unrelated things

✓ Create new and different experiments and scenarios

✓ Change, exaggerate and modify things

✓ Put things to new, other and different uses

✓ Remove or eliminate elements completely

✓ Reverse roles or turn things on their head

✓ Ask questions such as what if, why, and why not

✓ Use Brainstorming and Mind Mapping

✓ Make provocations and extract workable principles

✓ Copy or adapt ideas from different arenas

✓ Be willing to make mistakes and fail

✓ Have an open mind and delay making quick judgements

✓ Have a sense of humour and have fun

✓ Use visualization techniques to picture ideas

✓ Challenge and question the status quo

✓ Realise there are many possibilities not just ONE right answer

✓ Exercise the imagination and fully engage the senses

BRAINSTORMING AND
CREATIVITY RULES FOR GROUPS

"If everyone is thinking alike,
then somebody isn't thinking"

- George S. Patton

P roblem solving often takes place between a group of
people - whether in a friendship, relationship, marriage,
team or organization. Many groups and teams have
difficulty to collaborate or engage in creativity. Those who
are successful follow certain rules which will be shared
now. Firstly, it is important to create a relaxed and non-
judgmental atmosphere. When groups come together to
be creative, remove authority titles and allow for fun.
People must feel that their contributions are genuinely
appreciated, valued and that they will be listened to.

Use creative games, exercises, team activities and videos to help create the relaxed atmosphere. Make sure the group understands the problem and use creativity techniques such as SCAMPER, What If, and Random Words to generate new ideas. Write ALL the ideas down. Encourage wild and crazy combinations. Don't evaluate or judge ideas at this stage. Follow and share the items in the checklist with your problem solving group.

CHECKLIST FOR BRAINSTORMING AND GROUP CREATIVITY

✓ Make a dedicated time and space for creativity

✓ Create a relaxed atmosphere of equals without titles

✓ People must feel unafraid to share their ideas

✓ Use humour, creative exercises, games and video clips

✓ State the challenge clearly and concisely

✓ Identify and apply creativity techniques to it

✓ Quantity of ideas is important at this stage

✓ Delay judgement during the creative session

✓ Don't censor questions, instead listen and engage

✓ Work and build on the ideas of others

✓ Encourage diversity of thought and wild ideas

✓ Write all ideas down - give all a turn to contribute

✓ No arguments allowed - it's not about ego or who wins

✓ No discussions about evaluating ideas at this stage

"Creativity is inventing, experimenting, growing, taking risks, breaking rules, making mistakes, and having fun"

- Mary Lou Cook

THE SCAMPER TECHNIQUE

*"Progress comes from people who are
not satisfied with the way things are"*

The SCAMPER technique was developed and elaborated on by Alex Osborn and Michael Michalko respectively. It provides a very easy and practical approach to creativity by simply getting you to answer a number of specific questions about your problem to help you generate new ideas, insights and solutions. The reason this technique is so powerful is because it provides focus to creative thinking and takes it out of the subconscious and mystical and into the real and practical. Simply apply the questions to your challenge.

SCAMPER Template

CONCEPT	QUESTIONS
SUBSTITUTE AND STRETCH	Who or what else? What instead of what? What other ingredients, materials, process, pace, schedule, location, technology, approach, tone of voice, attitude? Etc...
COMBINE	What mixture can you combine? What elements or compounds? What materials? What processes? What ideas? What ingredients? What smell or textures? What roles? Etc...
ADAPT	What is this like? What does this remind you of? What ideas does this imply? What other areas can you learn and take from? What can be duplicated, copied or emulated? Etc...
MODIFY, MAGNIFY AND MINIFY	Different, new or improved? Change the meaning, sound, size, smell, form, twist, motion, colour, shape? Something more to add? Less or more time? What about frequency? Tougher or stronger? Higher or lower? Longer or shorter? Thicker or thinner? More or less Value? Different Ingredient? Multiply? What can you Exaggerate? Subtract? Make Bigger or Smaller? Condensed? Make into a miniature? Heavier or Lighter? Streamline? Split up? Understate or Overstate?
PUT TO ANOTHER USE	New ways to use as is? Other uses if you have it modified or changed completely?
ELIMINATE	Remove, omit, eliminate, take out, destroy? What is unnecessary? What is not important? What doesn't have value and can be discarded?
REVERSE AND REARRANGE	Transform positive into negative? What is the opposite? Flip it upside down, backwards, inside out? Interchange parts, materials? What other patterns? Different layout or sequence? Swap cause and effect? Reverse or change roles? Turn the tables?

GUIDE TO MIND MAPPING

*"Creativity is the power to connect
the seemingly unconnected"*

- William Plomer

M ind mapping is probably the most popular creativity and problem solving technique. Yet many people still don't know how to use it effectively. Mind mapping was developed by Tony Buzan. According to Buzan, mind maps work the same way your brain does, using images with networks of associations. The purpose of mind mapping is to generate, capture and organize random ideas and thinking into logical groups without worrying about order the way one does with a list. Mind mapping makes idea generating by association and images easy.

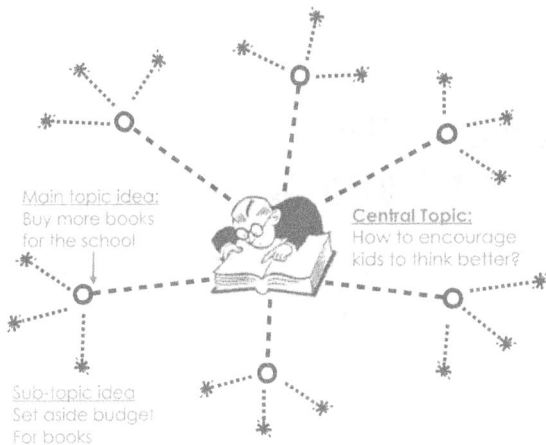

Main topic idea:
Buy more books
for the school

Central Topic:
How to encourage
kids to think better?

Sub-topic idea
Set aside budget
For books

MIND MAPPING CHECKLIST

✓ Clarify the topic you want to specifically mind map

✓ Put a word, picture or symbol at the centre of the page
and use it as heading to guide you in generating ideas

✓ Attach the main topic ideas to the central topic

✓ Attach the sub topic ideas under the main topic ideas

✓ Consider all the associations that can be made

✓ Use different colours to enhance memory by association

✓ Use the SCAMPER technique to prompt your thinking

✓ Make provocations, suggestions and use questioning

✓ All ideas are welcome at this stage so go wild

✓ If you are in a group allow others to build on your ideas

PROVOCATIONS -
WHAT IF AND WHY NOT

*"Focusing on things that are normally taken
for granted is a powerful source of creativity"*

- Edward de Bono

Good problem solvers are good at making provocations, asking questions and challenging assumptions and the status quo. In the creative problem solving sense, provocations are considered to be challenging and outrageous hypothetical statements that stretch your thinking. The techniques to create provocations are simply to state 'what if' or 'why not'. These techniques remind us that the world is full of possibilities. To apply, simply state 'what if...' - describe the imagined scenario in detail and consider the consequences that follow.

Provocations require you to delay your judgement and extract workable ideas. This requires you to be patient and to keep an open mind. For example you might say, 'what if the wheels of a car were like a chicken?' This is a provocation because what could wheels and chickens possibly have in common? To extract a principle from the provocation you might say that a chicken is sometimes white, so why not change the colours of the wheels (that are traditionally black in all vehicles) to white or to another colour altogether? Why not manufacture different coloured wheels to match different coloured cars? Continue to extract ideas until something feasible emerges. Use the 'What If' template in the Checklists and Templates section of the book to prompt your thinking further and to generate more creative ideas and solutions to problems.

CHECKLIST FOR MAKING PROVOCATIONS

✓ Keep an open mind and delay judgement
✓ Be patient as not all ideas will come fully formed
✓ Use 'what if' and 'why not' to start a provocation
✓ Be open to exploring new ideas
✓ Keep exploring until something workable emerges

"The power to rearrange the combinations of natural elements is the only creative power man possesses... Imagination is a faculty for rearranging the elements of reality to achieve human values"

- Ayn Rand

RANDOM WORD AND
FORCED CONNECTIONS

"Mystery is the catalyst for Imagination"

- J J Abrams

This is a powerful lateral-thinking technique that is very easy to use. All you have to do is have a bag full of cut up random words written on small pieces of paper, cardboard, magnets or any other material. Without looking, take out a word (or a number of random words) and apply it back to your problem. You can create new associations, combinations and scenarios that will stimulate new thinking and ideas. Alternatively, open a dictionary (newspaper or magazine) on a random page and choose a word or image and apply it back to your challenge.

Always ask or compare how the image or word relates to the problem. What is the metaphor? The idea of the forced connections method is to compare the problem with something else that has little or nothing in common with the problem and as a result to gain new insights. You can force a connection between almost anything, and get new insights for example:

✓ Insurance Companies and Mosquitoes
✓ Management Styles and Sports
✓ Lawyers and Sharks
✓ Jokes and Electricity Bills
✓ Firemen and Superheroes
✓ Quality and Steel
✓ Books and lobsters
✓ Phones and costumes

The list can go on and on. Remember to think metaphorically and consider how the random idea relates to your problem. Forcing relationships is one of the most powerful ways to develop new insights and new solutions. Use the random word technique to help you to create forced connections.

THE MORPHOLOGICAL ANALYSIS TECHNIQUE

*"Anything you can dream by the very nature
you can dream it makes it possible"*

- Leo F. Buscaglia

Coming up with new or improved ideas as possible solutions to problems couldn't be easier with the following technique. Morphological analysis is a technique which is simpler to understand and use than its name suggests. Firstly, clarify the focus, for example: To come up with an original design for a bicycle. Then list all the relevant characteristics of the problem, in this case the bicycle, such as, number of wheels, material of body, colour, desired speed, size and number of seats etc... Place all the characteristics in columns as headings on a page.

Morphological Analysis

CHARAC-TERISTICS	NO. OF WHEELS	MATERIAL OF BODY OR CHAIR	BODY COLOR	TOP SPEED	SIZE	NO. OF SEATS
CURRENT	2	Metal	Red	Up to 60 KM/H	Medium	1
	1	Plastic	Green	Up to 80 KM/H	Small	2
	3	Glass	Blue	Up to 100 KM/H	Large	3
	4	Wood	Purple	Up to 120 KM/H	The size of a chair	4
	5	Sponge	Yellow	Up to 140 KM/H	The size of a car	5

Under each heading list as many alternative characteristics as you can on top of the current reality. Once you are satisfied begin mixing, matching and combining the different characteristics in all the columns until you reach a workable idea. In the example above alone there are 15 625 possible combinations. Admittedly many combinations may not be practical or relevant but this technique certainly makes creating and exploring new possible combinations easy and fun. Use it in conjunction with the SCAMPER, 'What If', and 'A - Z Considerations' list. This technique can be used in any problem, just break down the focus into its characteristics and mix.

CONSIDER WHAT YOU CAN SIMPLIFY

*"Simplicity is the
ultimate sophistication"*

- Leonardo da Vinci

A great technique to generate new ideas, options and possibilities is to Simplify. Ask yourself what you can simplify. Simplify the challenge by separating the Necessary (N) elements from the Optional (O) ones. Problems are often blown out of proportion. People tend to develop elaborate strategies that are unnecessarily complicated. Why overcomplicate? Perhaps to feel more important, to look more clever or to show off to others and thus more likely to get that promotion, raise, appraisal, attention or deal. Though, this is not always the case.

Make no mistake, it is important to be as thorough as necessary but as the old saying goes "don't make it more complicated than it has to be." The results of unnecessary complexity are lost in translation and often end in confusion, misunderstanding and unnecessary conflicts and battles.

So when considering your problem, consider how you can simplify it. Ask yourself; is there is a simpler way to achieve success that will not compromise quality or the critical success factors? This requires a creative mind.

AS AN EXERCISE:

✓ List as many ways as you can that are simpler than your current approach to deal with the problem

✓ What steps can you remove from the process?

✓ List what is Necessary (N) and what is Optional (O)?

✓ Separate the (N) and (O) lists - see if you can solve the problem without or with less of the (O) optional elements

✓ Use the SCAMPER technique to SIMPLIFY

✓ Ask all the necessary questions

✓ Consider all the factors

✓ Check and challenge your assumptions

Consult the Equations, Recipes, Instructions and Experts

"Read the directions and directly you will be directed in the right direction"

Sometimes when looking for solutions you don't have to re-invent the wheel all the time. This world is full of inventors, designers, authors, programmers, architects, doctors, businessmen and business women. Ask yourself: How have others addressed this or a similar problem? What can you learn from others successes and failures? Who can you collaborate with or draw on that can make your efforts in addressing your particular problem so much easier? Some would say that this is not a creative approach to solving the problem, but that is not the point.

The point of this exercise is to learn from others and gain new perspectives. Once you have gained sufficient insights into how others have approached (succeeded or failed in) the same or similar problem, nothing stops you from applying creative techniques to your current problem and making creative decisions. At least you can say that you are aware of and learned lessons from others and the past and thus more prepared to address the problem.

Recipes, dosages, instructions, expert information, formulas and equations are recorded learning's and best practices of the past. Some are relevant today but others may no longer be and it is your responsibility to question which are which. But, there is no harm in learning from the lessons of the past to prevent and address the problems of the present and future, especially if those lessons are relevant to the current problem. Consider:

- ✓ Who are the experts and what do they say?
- ✓ What equations and calculations are available?
- ✓ What recipes and formulas are in existence?
- ✓ What do the instructions or prescribed dosage say?
- ✓ What does the encyclopedia, map or dictionary say?

THE KIDS TEMPLATE

*"Common Sense is not always
Common Practice"*

- Stephen R. Covey

C reative thinking can be enhanced by applying certain techniques and answering some questions. To focus your creativity in your problem solving effort use the KIDS template. All you need to do is simply answer what you should Keep Doing, Improve, Do Differently or Stop. Good problem solvers ensure that their creative efforts are focused, and this technique helps to identify focus clearly. You can use KIDS on your own or in a group when you solve problems. Use the template on the following page as a guideline.

KIDS Template

QUESTIONS	IDEAS
KEEP DOING	Continue to do as you are currently doing. It works so leave it alone and carry on doing what you are doing.
IMPROVE	Do what you are doing but do it better than you are doing it now. Define the quality standard clearly. If you want improvement then be specific about it.
DO DIFFERENTLY	Change direction and START something new or different. Be creative and think outside the box.
STOP	Stop what you are doing. It is not helping you or even worse it is causing you harm. List the things to stop.

KIDS is nothing short of common sense in practice. Focus your attention on one area at a time, generate ideas and list them in the separate categories. Whenever you feel you are running out of creative ideas, consider the KIDS template and reflect on where your focus has been so far. For example: your current focus and ideas may be only to improve, but what ideas can you generate to do something different? Use this technique in conjunction with the SCAMPER, 'What If' and 'How to improve or invent anything' list.

BUILD SCENARIOS, MAKE HYPOTHESES AND CREATE EXPERIMENTS

*"Knowledge arrives from failed
as well as successful experiments"*

Problem solving is not always an exact science. There are
many unknowns and uncertainties. That is why the good
problem solver builds scenarios, makes hypotheses and
creates experiments in order to test, and verify ideas.
A scenario is defined as *an imagined sequence of future
events*. A hypothesis is defined as *a suggested but un-
proven explanation based on assumption rather than
fact*. Making hypotheses is useful but they need to be
followed by experiments and tests in order to be proven
useful and usable.

An experiment is defined as *a test to provide evidence to prove or disprove a theory or hypothesis*. When looking for ideas and solutions to problems it is useful to design and build hypothetical scenarios and then experiment or build prototypes (models) to verify if the hypothesis or scenario is plausible. This scientific approach to problem solving requires creativity and objectivity.

Use the 'what if', 'why not' and SCAMPER techniques (discussed earlier) to create provocations - these will be the beginnings of scenarios and hypotheses - that will need to be tested - proved or disproved. This is a scientific approach. Science is defined as *the systematic study and knowledge of natural or physical phenomena*. Creativity is all about creating new scenarios, combinations, variations and experiments. Creativity, objectivity and science actually go hand in hand.

NOTE:

Use the guidelines on scenario building found in the characteristics section earlier on in this book.

"All life is an experiment The more experiments you make the better"

- Ralph Waldo Emerson

THE FRESH EYES TECHNIQUE

*"If the only tool you have is a hammer
you tend to see every problem as a nail"*

- Abraham Maslow

Whenever you think that you may be running out of ideas, use the Fresh Eyes technique. This technique requires that you do one of two things. The first thing you can do (randomly or purposefully) is to identify and ask how someone else would solve your problem for you. This 'someone else' could be a person, a company, an animal, a fictional character or an expert in a different job. The second thing you can do is to pretend that you are that person or thing yourself. This requires you to use your imagination. Use the following list to consider...

HOW WOULD A...

- ✓ A CEO, president or coach
- ✓ A banker or an accountant
- ✓ A marketer or a creative consultant
- ✓ A customer, a supplier or a philosopher
- ✓ A farmer, architect or an engineer
- ✓ A programmer, IT specialist, astronaut, pilot or child
- ✓ An alien, science fiction or mythical character
- ✓ Any animal - insect, bird, fish or mammal
- ✓ A writer, cartoonist, artist or a poet
- ✓ A time traveller from the future or past
- ✓ A theatre or film character
- ✓ A husband, wife or family member
- ✓ A famous sports man or woman
- ✓ Albert Einstein or another famous scientist
- ✓ Nelson Mandela or another famous historical figure
- ✓ A company like GE, Google, Nokia or Apple etc...

Perceive and solve your problem? You can always read about, ask or involve the elements listed above to find creative ways of solving your problem. In a group ask people to brainstorm or mind map the problem with Fresh Eyes to generate ideas in a completely new way.

"You always start with human needs, and you have to think creatively, there can be many ways to satisfy those needs"

- Stephen R. Covey

SPOT THE NEED, WANT OR OPPORTUNITY AND BE REMARKABLE

"The future belongs to those who see opportunities before they become obvious"

Problem solving requires that you become mindful of two areas. Yourself and the world around you. One of the greatest sources of creativity and innovation lies in identifying needs, wants and opportunities. How do you identify them? There are fundamentally two ways. Firstly you can simply ask people, customers or stakeholders what it is they want. You can use surveys, interviews, polls, service ratings or conversations to find out. The second approach is to observe people using the particular product or service and ask 'what is missing?'

The key to true creativity and innovation lies in aiming for remarkability. Remarkable is defined in the dictionary as *outstanding, worth noticing or making a remark about*. Truly creative ideas, innovations and solutions to problems stand out from the crowd of other ideas. They stand out in terms of their uniqueness and value. They are not merely a rehash of the past. Solutions that are remarkable are more noticeable than traditional ideas. To be remarkable you need to constantly think how to RENEW which stands for: Remarkable is Exceeding, Needs, Expectations and Wants that result in WOW. So how can you RENEW?

Checklist for Remarkability and Spotting Needs

✓ What are your stakeholders or customers suggesting, complaining about or complimenting you on?

✓ What changes in the (TESPGLM - see SWOT) could create opportunities or help you to solve your problems better?

✓ What are you missing that could help you solve your problems better - what could you improve or reinvent?

✓ What can you RENEW? Focus on what nobody else is?

✓ Find out what your stakeholders want or need by asking or observing them?

*"He has
a right to
criticise who
has a heart
to help"*

- Abraham Lincoln

THE JUDGEMENT RULES

"Small minds are the first to condemn great ideas"

Once you generate all the ideas you can, comes the time for judgement. At this stage you are going to evaluate and select the ideas that best meet your criteria for success within your limitations and boundaries. There are certain rules and considerations that you should follow or take into account to maximize the evaluation of the ideas. First of all, you need to be objective and not let your feelings get in the way of your judgement. You need to consider all the ideas carefully and then rank them. You should consider each idea individually and then compare.

THE JUDGEMENT RULES:

✓ Make a dedicated time and place
✓ Separate judgement from the creative process
✓ Consider other people's views
✓ Be a devil's advocate and find the loop holes or cracks
✓ See if you can kill the idea rationally
✓ Judge the ideas but never the person
✓ No arguments allowed only ordered debate
✓ Keep the critical success factors top of mind
✓ Use reason and objectivity
✓ Check your assumptions
✓ Quality of ideas is more important at this stage
✓ Listen carefully and don't be biased
✓ Don't jump to conclusions

Use the rules in the list above to guide your thinking and evaluation. The following section provides the essential considerations to take into account for judgement.

*"It is not Who is right but
What is right that is important"*

THE JUDGEMENT CONSIDERATIONS

"Emotion, positive or negative is far more seductive than thought but that doesn't make it right so use your reason as the first port of call"

When judging ideas, you have to essentially consider three things. Firstly, consider how well the ideas generated suit your original critical success factors. Secondly, consider if you (or your team) are capable to act upon the ideas now - either in terms of your access to resources or personal capability. Finally you have to consider how the ideas impact and relate to the external environments (TESPGLM - see SWOT section). The considerations list on the following page is the checklist you should use when judging any ideas.

When judging ideas...

- ✓ Consider all the risks, hazards and dangers
- ✓ Consider short, medium and long term consequences
- ✓ Consider the cost vs. benefit
- ✓ Consider the history - is this a new idea?
- ✓ Consider if it is appropriate
- ✓ Consider if you have all the required resources for success
- ✓ Consider if you have the technology and capability
- ✓ Consider all the forces for and against you
- ✓ Consider if it is logical and objective
- ✓ Consider if it meets the stakeholders' requirements
- ✓ Consider if it is moral, ethical, civil and legal
- ✓ Consider if it is sufficient given the required standard
- ✓ Consider other people's perspectives
- ✓ Consider both the facts and the feelings
- ✓ Consider the underlying beliefs, values or philosophy
- ✓ Consider pros and cons over time
- ✓ Consider the feasibility of success
- ✓ Consider the must have vs. nice to have
- ✓ Consider the impact of the idea - strong, medium or weak?
- ✓ Consider the timing - is it the right time
- ✓ Consider what is interesting about the idea
- ✓ Consider what can and cannot be tolerated

"Always judge on Character and Competence,
Never on Colour or Creed"

Sorting, Evaluating and Selecting

"All ideas pass through a stage where it is easy to rubbish them"

- Peter Honey

When you judge ideas it is always effective to sort them into categories before you begin evaluating. It becomes far easier to evaluate when you can see where the different ideas fall into. The DISK template is great technique for sorting and categorizing ideas. It gives you focus and saves you time. All you have to do is place all the generated ideas in similar categories and then evaluate them by moving them into the DISK template. Consider which ideas can be thrown away, used immediately, require elaboration or can be used later.

A simple way to evaluate ideas is to rank them from best to worst by placing a number from 1 to 5 where:

✓ 1 = worst and
✓ 5 = best

Simply place a number next to each idea that is useful and rank all of them accordingly. This is also a good way to evaluate ideas in a group. Ask all members of a group to individually rank the ideas by placing a number next to each one and then as a group you can decide how to go forward. Another technique to evaluate ideas is to let the members of the group evaluate the ideas individually in private and then provide you with their responses anonymously. This way, there is a better chance that the evaluations are honest and not fearful.

Before you begin evaluating ideas, sort all ideas into similar categories and then decide in which section of the DISK template they fall into. For example, all marketing ideas in one category, all customer service ideas in another category and all product ideas in a third category. Once you have all your ideas in all categories use the DISK template to go forward.

The DISK Template

CONCEPT	DETAILS
DUSTBIN	Place all the ideas that you want to throw away or will never use in here.
IMPROVE	Place all ideas that you see potential in but that require elaboration before they can be used here.
SHELF AWAY	Place all ideas that have value but cannot be used at the moment but may be used in future here.
KICK OFF	Place all ideas that are perfect the way they are and can be used and acted upon here.

Ideas that you don't want to use go in the Dustbin. Ideas that are valuable but you can't do anything about at this moment can be Shelved Away for future reference. Ideas that are incomplete but have potential go into the Improve section for further elaboration. Finally, ideas that are fully formed and can be acted upon straightaway go into the Kick Off section.

"What good is aim if you don't let loose the arrow"

THE GAP TEMPLATE

> *"Knowing is not enough,
> you must take action"*
>
> - Tony Robbins

Taking action is the most essential part of problem solving. Good problem solvers take the necessary action steps to overcome whatever problem they are facing. Poor problem solving occurs when you fail to take action. The reasons for not taking action include: fear, lack of focus, motivation, creativity or resources. The sections that follow discuss the important considerations for writing action plans and taking action. To succeed in taking action you should take note of certain rules. Consider the elements in the GAP template to take action.

The GAP Template

CONCEPT	CONSIDERATIONS
DESCRIBE	What is the background of the problem and where are you now? Look at the problem from all perspectives.
DESTINATION	Where do you want to be? What does success look like? Describe the destination or success factors clearly.
DETAILS	What information do you have to carefully take into consideration to solve the problem?
DESIGN	What are the steps that need to be taken to get from where you are now to where you want to be?
DELEGATE	Who are the people who you can call on to assist you to solve the problem?
DANGERS	Who are the people, disruptions or obstacles who you should avoid or overcome to solve the problem?
DEADLINES	When are you planning to start and finish? When are the deadlines that the problem has to be solved by?

"Clarify what you will have to go through to get to where you want to be"

THE NEW SMARTER GOALS TEMPLATE

"A goal is a dream with a deadline"

When you go about solving problems it is always a good idea to set goals clearly and include deadlines. The SMARTER goals template on the following page provides you with an effective guideline to set goals. Poor problem solvers don't set goals clearly or effectively. Their goals are like hazy targets. Good problem solvers understand that a clear a goal, like a clear target, is more likely to be accomplished. Make sure to check your goal against the SMARTER goals template the next time you solve a problem.

SMARTER Goals Template

CONCEPT	QUESTIONS
SPECIFIC	Specific goals have a better chance of getting done than general ones. For goals to be specific they need to answer all the questions: WHO (is required or involved) WHAT (do I want to achieve and in what order of importance) WHERE (location) WHEN (starting date and deadline) WHICH (requirements and constraints) WHY (Specific purpose, reason or benefits of the goal) HOW (Cost, length, duration, numbers, method...)
MEASURABLE	Set specific criteria for monitoring and measuring the progress of each goal. When you measure your progress, you stay on track and reach your target dates. To check if the goal is measurable, ask and answer questions like: How long, how much and how will I know when my goal has been achieved?
ATTITUDE AND ATMOSPHERE	On the road to accomplish any goal you need to adopt a positive attitude and create a positive atmosphere in the environment you are going to be achieving the goal in. Ask yourself: do I (or my colleagues) have the right attitude to achieve the goal and do I have the right atmosphere to do it? If not ask yourself WHY and WHAT can be done.
REALISTIC AND RATIONAL	To know if a goal is realistic requires you to determine if you or others have accomplished the same or similar goal in the past. To ask yourself what conditions would have to exist to accomplish this goal? Is the technology available to realise the goal? Is it objective? Is it possible given the current barriers that exist and can those be overcome?
TRAINING AND TOOLS	Consider the tools, training and accreditation you need to have in order to address the goal and solve the problem. Consider What training and tools you currently have and what you still need in order to move forward.
EXPECTATIONS AND EXPERTS	Does this goal fulfil all my or my stakeholders expectations? If not then what needs to be changed to fulfil them (Use the SCAMPER template)? Consider which experts you can connect with to help you accomplish your goals.
RESPONSIBLE	To address any goal and solve any problem you must take responsibility and accountability for your actions and the consequences of those actions.

"*The general who wins the battle makes many calculations in his temple before the battle is fought. The general who loses makes a few calculations beforehand*"

- Sun Tzu

OVERCOMING PROCRASTINATION

"Great things are not done by impulse, but by a series of small things brought together"

- Vincent Van Gogh

W hat is procrastination? Why do people do it? Surely, if you knew what you wanted to do, how to do it, and why you were doing it, procrastination would not occur. Unfortunately, many people spend their time delaying goals, plans, and even their dreams, all in the name of procrastination. The dictionary describes procrastination as *postponement of action, deferring, delaying, prolonging, stalling, and waiting*. The reason many people procrastinate primarily comes down to fear. The types of fear vary, here a the typical examples.

It could be fear of failure, ridicule, success, looking stupid, making mistakes, or looking childish. In addressing any problem there is a chance that you could make mistakes. Usually many people, in our mistake-averse culture, will continue to procrastinate. Some people continue to procrastinate because they do not believe that they have it in them to succeed. They hold themselves back because of a limiting self-image.

This limiting and fearful self-image is something that you need to discard if you are to become a better problem solver. Nike's famous advertising logo puts it simply "Just Do It." This is a very powerful statement. Forget about failure. Forget about being perfect. Forget about making mistakes. Just focus on clarifying the problem and on addressing the solution as best you can.

This reminds me of the film Patch Adams. In one scene, Patch (played by Robin Williams) is sitting with another patient in a mental institution, who teaches him a powerful life lesson in solving problems.

The patient tells him the following nugget of wisdom "If you only focus on the problem, you won't see the solution. So never (just) focus on the problem." I love this statement because it forces Patch to see past the problem and into the solution. This inspires Patch to leave the institution and take responsibility for his life. Similarly, when you procrastinate, what you are really doing is focusing on the problem and letting it overwhelm you.

What you should do instead is understand the problem clearly, but then shift your attention and energy towards generating solutions and taking action. Don't try to swallow it all at once or you will choke. Cut up your problem into smaller tasks, set deadlines and resolve to address it step by step.

"...If not now then when..."

CHECKLIST TO STOP PROCRASTINATING

✓ Stop trying to be perfect

✓ Don't leave it to the last minute

✓ Experiment with options and don't be afraid to fail

✓ Practice practice practice

✓ Check your expectations - are they realistic?

✓ Break down tasks into smaller tasks

✓ Write down deadlines and stick to them

✓ Don't be afraid to make mistakes in order to learn

✓ Learn from your and others past mistakes

✓ Catch yourself procrastinating and be mindful

✓ Clearly identify, write down and burn your excuses

✓ Keep your goals top of mind

✓ Remember that action is worryings worst enemy

✓ Act as though it were impossible to fail

*"The wise does at once
what the fool does at last"*

TAKE ACTION AND HAVE A BACKUP PLAN

*"Action is the foundational
key to all success"*

- Pablo Picasso

G ood problem solvers follow through with their plans
and take action. Often one of the causes of poor problem
solving comes down to not taking action. A problem may
be defined and understood. You may have generated
ideas and selected the best ones but if you don't take
action then it was all for nothing. Reading a book like this
one is not a substitute for taking action. You must be
willing to follow through if you are to be a successful
problem solver. It is also a good idea to take precautions
and have a backup plan.

Backup plans are the result of asking what if and scenario thinking. If things change or don't work out the way you had planned in your problem solving approach then a backup plan would be the first thing to rely on. You don't have to have just one backup plan, but as many as you like within your constraints (time, money, people, materials). Following through on action plans and having backup plans ready requires mindfulness, scenario thinking, discipline and the ability to keep your eyes on the ball. You have to be up to date with the problem and the changes in the world. As a successful problem solver you must be willing to exercise discipline, follow through on your plans and take action.

BACKUP PLAN CHECKLIST

- ✓ Consider what could go wrong
- ✓ Consider what can be done to prevent it
- ✓ Consider what you will do if things do go wrong
- ✓ Consider different scenarios and their consequences
- ✓ Consider your different responses to those scenarios
- ✓ Consider your SWOT and the (TESPGLM) environments
- ✓ Consider all the forces for and against you
- ✓ Consider your goals, priorities, deadlines and resources

MONITOR PROGRESS AND RECORD LESSONS FOR THE FUTURE

"The unexamined life is not worth living"

- Socrates

Since problem solving is not a static activity things are bound to change at one point or another. So when you are following through on your problem solving action plan make sure to monitor your progress. Are you accomplishing the results you are looking for? Are things going according to plan? What have you accomplished? How much do you still have to go? Monitoring progress is effective at helping you get a clearer understanding of how far you are from where you want to be. It is mindful to monitor progress.

Monitoring is an essential part of problem solving because it will inform you of any changes that may occur and help you consider what you should do about them. In every problem solving effort you will make some mistakes and learn certain lessons. Poor problem solvers are not mindful. They don't pay attention to the mistakes and lessons and as a result repeat the same ones over and over again. Good problem solvers take note of mistakes and lessons and write them down to remember them for future problem solving efforts.

If you don't learn from the past, expect to experience a lifetime of repeating the same mistakes over and over again. Some people have a hard time addressing their problems, learning from their mistakes and changing their habits and behaviours. If this is the case with you get a mentor, coach or a professional that can guide you.

"History, despite its wrenching pain, cannot be unlived, but if faced with courage, need not be lived again"

- Maya Angelou

Always consider if your current problem solving approach is helping you to solve the problem. Yes, no or unsure? If YES then continue, if NO then stop and change direction, if UNSURE then consult an expert.

CHECKLIST TO MONITOR

✓ Decide how often you need to monitor your action plan

✓ Review your critical success factors regularly

✓ Talk to your stakeholders regularly

✓ Check that everything is up to quality standard

✓ Use Interviews, polls, surveys, formal and informal talks

✓ Regularly compare actual to the ideal situation

✓ Check budget and resources - are you within or over

✓ Consider what you may be missing

CHECKLIST TO REFLECT FOR THE FUTURE

✓ What should you stop, keep doing, do better or differently

✓ What went well and what went poorly - learn from it

✓ Record the lessons in a place that will be easy to review

✓ Make the lessons visible for others to learn from and use

"Where observation is concerned,
chance favours only the prepared mind"

- Pasteur

"When a wise man is advised of his errors, he will reflect on and improve his conduct. When his misconduct is pointed out, a foolish man will not only disregard the advice but rather repeat the same error"

- Budda

A GUIDE TO THE CHECKLISTS AND TEMPLATES

"Truth always expresses itself with the greatest simplicity"

- Pierre Schmidt

The following section contains a number of checklists and templates that are essential for problem solving success. These checklists and templates will help you focus your thinking, enhance your creativity, make you mindful of what to consider, help you evaluate consequences and highlight all the things that you should avoid. These checklists and templates are indispensable, I suggest that you print them out as brochures or posters, use them and apply them to every problem you or your team face.

The first template is the 'How to Invent or Improve anything' list. This comprehensive list can be used to prompt creative thinking or help identify focus areas for improvement. The 'What if' list is full of provocations and can be used to provoke your thinking for creativity and innovation. The 'A - Z Considerations' list can be used to prompt your thinking as to what you should be considering throughout the problem solving process from what to focus on to what action to take. The 'Consequences' template can help you distinguish between the positive and negative consequences of your ideas, beliefs, thoughts, feelings, decisions or actions over time, specifically the short, medium and long term. The 'Don't list' explicitly highlights attitudes, feelings and behaviours you should mindfully avoid to become a better problem solver. The final three checklists focus on poor thinking habits and behaviours that result in poor problem solving. 'Logical Fallacies' are false beliefs and unsound reasoning that you should avoid if you are to become a better problem solver. Be mindful of the 'Creativity Killers' and finally be wary of the elements that 'Cause Failure' in problem solving.

The IMPROVE and INVENT ANYTHING List

IMPROVE AND INVENT ANYTHING...	
ADD OR SUBTRACT FUNCTIONS OR USES	INTROSPECT ON EVERYTHING FROM START TO FINISH
APPLY TO A DIFFERENT OR NEW USE	LEARN FROM BEST PRACTICES
ASSESS LIMITATIONS OF THE CURRENT REALITY	ADAPT FROM MYTHOLOGY, FICTION AND SCI-FI
COPY OR ADAPT FROM SOMEWHERE ELSE	LOOK AT UNMET AND UNEXPRESSED NEEDS
CAN YOU MAKE IT CHEAPER OR FREE	WHAT ELSE CAN BE ADDED OR SUBTRACTED
CAN YOU MAKE IT EASIER TO LEARN AND USE	MAKE IT AUTOMATED OR RELIANT ON SUPERVISION
CAN YOU MAKE IT EASIER TO UNDERSTAND	MAKE IT CLEARER OR MORE FOCUSED
CAN YOU MAKE IT INTERACTIVE AND DYNAMIC	MAKE IT EASY, INTERESTING AND FUN
CAN YOU MAKE IT PORTABLE OR POWERFUL	MAKE IT FASTER OR PERFORM BETTER
CAN YOU MAKE IT QUIETER OR LOUDER	MAKE IT FUNNIER OR MORE SERIOUS
CREATE A BETTER PROMOTION OR PACKAGING	MAKE IT LIGHTER OR HEAVIER IN WEIGHT
CAN YOU MAKE IT SMALLER OR LARGER	MAKE IT LOOK BETTER OR MORE COMFORTABLE
CHANGE DIRECTION OR INDUSTRY	MAKE IT MORE ACCEPTABLE TO OTHERS
REARRANGE, REPLACE OR RENEW PARTS	MAKE IT MORE DURABLE AND RELIABLE
COPY OR ADAPT IDEAS FROM OTHER INDUSTRIES	MAKE IT MORE EFFICIENT SO THERE IS LESS WAITING
IMPROVE ACCURACY, CAPACITY OR ELEGANCE	MAKE IT MORE / LESS CONNECTED OR DEPENDENT
IMPROVE THE SERVICE OR MAKE IT EXCLUSIVE	MAKE IT WORLD CLASS OR UNIQUE
SEE COMPLAINTS, COMPLIMENTS & COMMENTS	WHAT CAN YOU CUSTOMIZE OR PERSONALIZE
IMPROVE EMOTIONAL OR SENSORY APPEAL	MAKE IT PROVOCATIVE OR CHANGE THE STYLE
IMPROVE FLEXIBILITY AND VERSATILITY	PROVIDE BETTER PERFORMANCE
IMPROVE OR PROMOTE HEALTH AND SAFETY	REDUCE COST TO MANUFACTURE OR PRODUCE
IMPROVE PSYCHOLOGICAL APPEAL	REDUCE FEAR TO OWN OR USE
USE OR ADD A METAPHOR OR SYMBOL	REDUCE OR ELIMINATE NEGATIVE SIDE EFFECTS
CHANGE SHAPE, DESIGN, THEME, PATTERN	SAVE TIME, MONEY, AND EFFORT
IMPROVE THE TOTAL CUSTOMER EXPERIENCE	SEE THE BIG PICTURE AND CONSIDER THE FUTURE
INCREASE OR DECREASE IN VALUE OR PRICE	SET FOCUS ON THE LONG TERM GOALS
INCREASE OR DECREASE SIZE, SCALE OR VARIETY	SIMPLIFY OR REMOVE COMPLEXITY
INCREASE EFFICIENCY AND EFFECTIVENESS	WHAT CAN YOU COMBINE OR INTEGRATE
INCREASE SPEED OF DELIVERY	WHAT FUNCTIONS CAN YOU SEPARATE

The WHAT IF List

WHAT IF (IT / IS)...	
YOU USE A HAMMER OR SOME TOOL	CREATED BY AN ALIEN, MAGICIAN OR A FAIRY
COLORFUL OR COLORLESS	HAD A FAVORITE BOOK, FOOD OR FRIEND
LIKE A MAGNET, GLUE OR POST IT NOTE	MADE FROM A DIFFERENT MATERIAL
FASTER, FATTER, FLATTER, OR FRAGRANT	HAD A HOBBY, HOUSE OR HAIRCUT
YOU REARRANGE IT PARTIALLY OR COMPLETELY	YOU WRITE A JOKE ABOUT IT
YOU SLEPT ON IT LIKE A BED	YOU INCREASE OR DECREASE THE VALUE
MADE OF CHEESE OR ANY OTHER FOOD	HAD A NAME OR AN ATTITUDE
A ROBOT OR ON REMOTE CONTROL	THERE WAS VERY LITTLE OR NO TIME LEFT
HAS A TEXTURE OR FLAVOR	HAD FRIENDS OR CAN MAKE FRIENDS
YOU CAN ADD OR SUBTRACT FEATURES	LIKES PRESENTS OR SPORTS
BOUNCES, BROKEN OR BIGGER	LIKE A STAR SIGN, CAR, SUPERHERO OR ANIMAL
COMES FROM ANOTHER CULTURE OR PLANET	HAD A THEME SONG OR COULD DRINK FIRE
YOU CHANGED THE PACKAGING SOMEHOW	LIKE A CALENDAR, CHEMICAL, OR DRINK
MANUAL OR AUTOMATIC	LIKE A MOVIE, SITCOM OR SONG
YOU HAD A PARTY OR CELEBRATION	LIKE A TIMETABLE, CHEMICAL, OIL OR WATER
CAN DO SOMETHING DIFFERENT	MADE OF CHOCOLATE OR VANILLA
CAN MOVE OR NEEDS A REMOTE CONTROL	MADE OF GOLD OR SILVER
EVOKES EMOTIONS - WHAT ARE THEY	WAS LIKE A PIRATE, DINOSAUR OR CARTOON
EXISTS IN THE FUTURE OR HAS IN THE PAST	WEARS CLOTHES, HATS OR SHOES
LOOKS LIKE A VIDEO GAME OR MACHINE	MAKES A NOISE OR COMPLETELY SILENT
COMES WITH ACCESSORIES OR BATTERIES	SLOWER, SMALLER, SMELLIER OR A SWEETER
INVENTED BY A CHILD OR MONEY IS NO ISSUE	YOU CHANGE MATERIALS OR INGREDIENTS
WIDER, WARMER, WITTIER OR WELCOMING	YOU COMBINE IT WITH SOMETHING ELSE
YOU COULD WRITE OR DRAW IN OR ON IT	YOU COULD ALSO DRINK OR EAT IT
YOU DESIGN FOR THE NEXT GENERATION	YOU BREAK IT APART AND REBUILD IT
YOU DESIGN FOR THE PREVIOUS GENERATION	MADE OF A DIFFERENT MATERIAL
YOU LOOK AT IT FROM ANOTHER ANGLE	THICKER OR THINNER - VISIBLE OR INVISIBLE
THE COMPETITION CREATED IT	IT WAS A BALLOON, SUBMARINE OR JET

The A - Z CONSIDERATIONS List

CONSIDER THESE AND WHAT ELSE...	
ACCOUNTING AND TAX	LANGUAGES - BARRIERS AND TRANSLATORS
AVAILABILITY - OF ALL STAKEHOLDERS	LEGAL - SUPPORT, POLICIES AND REGULATIONS
ARRANGEMENTS - E.G. SEATING	LIGHTING, HEATING AND AIR CONDITIONING
ATTITUDE AND BEHAVIOUR	LOANS, LOCATION, LOGISTICS AND LICENSE...
BUDGET AND BREAK EVEN	MARKETING, PROMOTION AND ADVERTISING
CAPACITY AND COSTS	MEDICINE, MATERIALS AND EQUIPMENT
COMBINATIONS - FORMULAS AND RECIPES	MEASUREMENT - LENGTH, WIDTH AND HEIGHT...
COMMUNICATIONS - ONLINE, BROCHURES ETC...	MOTIVATION, MEMBERSHIPS AND PARTNERSHIPS
(SWOT) COMPETITORS AND YOURS	MONEY - START UP, OPERATING COST
COMPLIMENTS AND COMPLAINTS - FEEDBACK	NECESSARY NEGOTIATIONS
CONTRACTS, CONDIMENTS AND COLORS	NUMBERS - ACCOUNT, TELEPHONE, VOLUMES...
CONSTRUCTION AND DIAGRAMS	ORDER - OF ACTION, OF PROJECTS OR PRIORITIES
CREATIVITY, EXPERIMENTS AND INNOVATION	OPINIONS, PRINTING, PAYMENTS AND PERCEPTIONS
CULTURES AND RELIGIONS (ACCOMMODATE)	(ALL REQUIRED) PEOPLE E.G. EMPLOYEES...
CURRENCY, CONVERSION, COSTS	(CURRENT) POLICIES, PROCESSES OR PROCEDURES
CUTLERY, FOOD AND SPICES	PHILOSOPHY, PRINCIPLES, MORALS AND ETHICS
DATES - IMPORTANT, STARTING AND ENDING...	PROJECT SCOPE - FOCUS, COST, TIME, PEOPLE
DESIGN OR DECORATIONS E.G. PAINT OR PLANTS	PURPOSE - VISION, MISSION AND VALUES
DIRECTORIES, DIRECTIONS - MAPS	QUALITY STANDARDS AND REPUTATION
DISCOUNTS OR PRICE SPECIALS	RESEARCH AND DEVELOPMENT (INVENTION)
DRESS CODE AND CLOTHING	RISKS, REWARDS, SECURITY AND INSURANCE
EDUCATION AND ACCREDITATION	SYSTEMS AND TECHNOLOGY REQUIRED
ENERGY - REQUIREMENTS AND COSTS	SALARIES, SERVICE, SPEED (AND FREQUENCY)
ENTERTAINMENT - GAMES, MUSIC, DANCING...	SMELL, TASTE AND SPICE - INCLUDE ALL SENSES
EXPERT EXPERIENCE (PAST AND PRESENT)	STRUCTURE, SCHEDULES AND STRATEGY
(THE) ENVIRONMENT AND EXPIRY DATES	STAKEHOLDERS EXPECTATIONS AND CONCERNS
FAIRNESS, FORMS AND DOCUMENTS	SUPPLIERS, SERVICES, STORAGE AND SYSTEMS
FOOD - STARTERS, MAIN, DESSERT OR SNACKS	THEMES - MODERN, CLASSIC, OR TRADITIONAL...
FORCES - POSITIVE, NEGATIVE, FOR OR AGAINST	TIME - SHORT, MEDIUM AND LONG TERM
HEALTH, HYGIENE AND HIRING	THEORY, TOOLS, TRAINING AND TRANSPORTATION
INFORMATION, KNOWLEDGE AND LEARNING	VEHICLES, VISIBILITY, VENUES AND WAREHOUSES

The CONSEQUENCES Template

BELIEFS VALUES IDEAS DECISIONS ACTIONS	CONSEQUENCES		TIME
	POSITIVE (+) BENEFIT OR VALUE	NEGATIVE (-) COST OR RISK	
e.g. To purchase a new sports car			IMMEDIATE (NOW)
			SHORT TERM (WEEK - YEAR)
			MEDIUM TERM (1 - 8 YEARS)
			LONG TERM (8 - 80 YEARS)
TOTAL WEIGHT or SCORE			

People have trouble seeing the consequences of actions beyond the immediate. Seeing short term consequences is sometimes done but most people do not connect their actions with medium and long term consequences. Use this template to visualize and evaluate the positive or negative consequences of your beliefs, values, ideas, decisions or actions over the short and long term. For example: Consider an action you wish to take then consider the positive and negative consequences over time.

The DON'T List

DON'T...	
PROCRASTINATE, DELAY OR BE LAZY	IGNORE OR LOSE SIGHT OF REALITY
BE AFRAID, WORRIED, STRESSED OR DEPRESSED	HAVE UNREALISTIC EXPECTATIONS
ARGUE UNNECESSARILY JUST TO BE RIGHT	BE PARANOID OR SUPERSTITIOUS
BE FRUSTRATED OR LOSE YOUR TEMPER	BE A BULLY, HARM OR OPPRESS OTHERS
WASTE - TIME, MONEY, ENERGY, RESOURCES...	BE IRRESPONSIBLE OR GAMBLE
STEREOTYPE OR GENERALIZE	FOLLOW BLINDLY WITHOUT QUESTIONING
BE JEALOUS, BIASED OR UNFAIR	LIE, MANIPULATE OR DECEIVE
BE NERVOUS OR PANIC	BE FAKE, IMMORAL OR CORRUPT
BE HYPOCRITICAL OR ARROGANT	LEAVE IT TO THE LAST MINUTE
BLOW THINGS OUT OF PROPORTION	EMOTIONALLY BLACKMAIL OTHERS
JUMP TO QUICK CONCLUSIONS OR PREJUDGE	REGRET THE PAST INSTEAD LEARN FROM IT
ONLY RELY ON INTUITION OR GUT FEEL	LOSE PATIENCE WITH YOURSELF OR OTHERS
BLAME OR SCAPEGOAT OTHERS	BE STUBBORN OR CLOSE MINDED
LET YOUR HABITS RUN AND RUIN YOUR LIFE	GET DISTRACTED OR SIDE TRACKED
BE FOOLISH, DEPENDENT OR BE A VICTIM	BE INCONSISTENT OR CONTRADICTORY
BE OBNOXIOUS OR DISRESPECTFUL	HAVE DOUBLE STANDARDS
OVERCOMPLICATE THE PROBLEM	JUST COMPLAIN WITHOUT DOING SOMETHING
IGNORE OR AVOID THE PROBLEM	BE CRITICAL WITHOUT SUGGESTING ALTERNATIVES
EMBARRASS OR BE RUDE	JUST SPECULATE WITHOUT CHECKING FACTS
BE INSENSITIVE OR INCONSIDERATE	LET YOUR EGO OR PRIDE GET INVOLVED

"Worrying is like a rocking chair, it gives you something to do but doesn't get you anywhere"

If you can't help others at least don't hurt them"

- The Dalai Lama

AVOID LOGICAL FALLACIES

Logical fallacies result from ignoring facts and replacing objectivity with assumption, prejudice and generalisation:

* Judging, accepting or rejecting an idea by the goodness or badness of its source and not on its own merits
* Thinking that if one idea is right then the other MUST be wrong - what if both are wrong or there is a different option?
* Ignoring the argument and focusing only on the person
* The fact that an idea is popular, in the media, or been around for a long time is not evidence that it is right or true
* Rejecting an idea as entirely false because the argument offered for it is insufficient or inadequate
* Instead of dealing with objective facts there is an appeal to your pity or a threat of consequences from an authority (religious or political) in order to influence or force you
* Dealing with something as true because it was true in the past even though it may not be true anymore
* Completely replacing facts and objectivity with intuition
* Assuming that everything is already perfect the way it is now and nothing needs to change
* Accepting an idea or argument because you like a person or thing even if the logic or facts are wrong or inconsistent
* Maliciously diverting attention away from the real problems
* Assuming what is good for the one is good for everyone else
* Exaggerating an argument to ridiculous conclusions and then judging the argument or person on your exaggerations
* Generalisations, prejudices, assumptions and racism e.g. thinking that the characteristics of a certain individual or group (e.g. race) is representative of all of them
* Read more about logical fallacies and be sure to challenge and avoid them and catch yourself or others making them

THE CREATIVITY KILLERS

- ✗ It can't be done
- ✗ It costs too much
- ✗ It's against company policy
- ✗ It's too much trouble to change
- ✗ It's too radical a change
- ✗ Not enough help
- ✗ That will run up our overhead
- ✗ That's not my job
- ✗ The staff will never buy it
- ✗ The managers don't want to risk it
- ✗ We don't have the time
- ✗ We tried that before
- ✗ Don't rock the boat
- ✗ Good thought but impractical
- ✗ I don't like the idea it's stupid
- ✗ If it isn't broke, don't fix it
- ✗ It isn't in the budget
- ✗ It's impossible
- ✗ It's too much work
- ✗ Quit dreaming
- ✗ We've always done it this way
- ✗ You can't teach an old dog new tricks

"Nothing is harder to open
than a closed mind"

THE CAUSES OF FAILURE

- ✗ Lack of focus or focus on the wrong things
- ✗ Having unrealistic expectations
- ✗ Not putting your priorities first
- ✗ Trying to juggle too many things at once
- ✗ Not considering all things that need to be considered
- ✗ Not having the right or enough skill or the right attitude
- ✗ Not having the right or enough resources
- ✗ Not having the right, enough or credible information
- ✗ Not enough ideas or insufficient creativity
- ✗ Not being prepared, not practicing or rehearsing
- ✗ Making illogical assumptions (logical fallacies)
- ✗ Being impatient and losing your temper
- ✗ Not having self confidence or courage
- ✗ Not thinking about the consequences of your actions
- ✗ Not learning from your own and others past mistakes
- ✗ Blowing things out of proportion
- ✗ Lying to yourself or others and not having integrity
- ✗ Causing harm or pain to others purposefully
- ✗ Not communicating clearly and not listening
- ✗ Being rude with others
- ✗ Not being genuine, objective or creative
- ✗ Fear and lack of motivation

Fear is Fresh Energy
Against Reason

"*Keep away from people who try to belittle your ambitions. Small people always do that, but the really Great make you feel that you, too, can become great*"

- Mark Twain

PROBLEM SOLVING SUMMARY

"Have you got a problem? Do what you can where you are with what you've got"

- Theodore Roosevelt

Problem solving is both a mind set and a process. Good problem solvers adopt positive and responsible attitudes and behaviours. They focus on clarifying what the problem is. They apply their minds and generate creative ideas. They think critically, evaluate and select the best options and then (most importantly) they take action. The following page contains a problem solving summary template. This template contains the 27 P's to consider when solving just about any problem and summarizes the key points of problem solving.

PROBLEM SOLVING SUMMARY

- ✓ Don't PANIC and act PROFESSIONALLY
- ✓ Consider your PHILOSOPHY, beliefs and values carefully
- ✓ Choose a POSITIVE attitude and act responsibly
- ✓ PRIORITIZE the problems in your life
- ✓ Focus and define the current PROBLEM clearly and simply
- ✓ Break down the problem into manageable PARTS
- ✓ Consider all the PREREQUISITES for success
- ✓ Consider your POWER and POTENTIAL
- ✓ Consider the POTHOLES or challenges that you may face
- ✓ Consider all the PEOPLE to include and their PERSPECTIVES
- ✓ Get all the information and challenge the PRESUMPTIONS
- ✓ PRESENT and communicate clearly and Listen thoroughly
- ✓ Consider the PROCEDURES that need to be observed
- ✓ Be creative and generate new ideas and POSSIBILITIES
- ✓ PONDER and select ideas that match the criteria for success
- ✓ Write a PRACTICAL action PLAN
- ✓ PREPARE all the necessary resources
- ✓ Don't PROCRASTINATE or leave it to the last minute
- ✓ PROTOTYPE and test your ideas and make improvements
- ✓ Take PRECAUTIONS, Take Action and Monitor Progress
- ✓ Learn to be PATIENT and PERSEVERE in your efforts
- ✓ Learn and record lessons from PAST problem solving efforts

CLOSING COMMENTS

It has been quite a journey for me to write this book. Working through literally hundreds of articles, research papers and books I've applied my mind to create a practical and comprehensive problem solving manual. Now that you have finished going through the book, I suggest you use this book as a manual and keep it close by. Catch yourself in a bad attitude, be mindful and ask what attitude you should replace it with. If you are running out of ideas use the creativity section. If you are unsure of what to consider when writing action plans refer to that section of the book. Some of the key lessons to remember in solving just about any problem include:

✓ Be mindful, think and see the big picture
✓ Create a dedicated time to address the problem
✓ Write your problem and actions down
✓ Clarify the focus
✓ Think before you act
✓ Separate creativity from judgement
✓ Overcome what is holding you back
✓ Take action and deal with the problem step by step
✓ Learn from your past mistakes
✓ Overcome your negativity or that of others

READ THESE AUTHORS

To enrich your problem solving thinking I strongly recommend you look up the following authors and review their works. All of them can be found with a Google search or a visit to your local or online bookstore.

- ✓ Edward De Bono
- ✓ Tom Peters
- ✓ Seth Godin
- ✓ Ruth Tearle
- ✓ Peter Drucker
- ✓ Stephen R. Covey
- ✓ Tony Buzan
- ✓ Anthony Robbins
- ✓ John C. Maxwell
- ✓ Leo F. Buscaglia
- ✓ Ayn Rand
- ✓ Zig Ziglar
- ✓ Daniel Goleman
- ✓ Patrick Dixon
- ✓ Michael Michalko

ACKNOWLEDGEMENTS

This book wouldn't have been possible without the inspiration and support from a number of important people in my life. Thank you Ruth and Itha for being the muses and coaches in my life, the fire that you've lit inside me will live on forever. Thank you to my parents and sister - Leonid, Maya and Lara - who have in their own weird and wonderful ways, taught me some of the most important lessons in life and made me a better person and problem solver. Thank you to my best friend Vova, you've given me your support and tools and reminded me to take things step by step and write things down - well here I've done it in black and white - Your friendship is priceless to me. Last but not least I would like to thank my wife and the love of my life Simone. Thank you for standing by me through the good times and bad times, I love you so much and always will.

ABOUT THE AUTHOR

Greg Z. Fainberg is Director of CEXINO Consulting. CEXINO stands for Customer Experience Innovation. This consultancy helps Individuals and Organizations become CEXii – Customer Experience Intelligent and Innovative. Greg Z. Fainberg is a life coach, innovation and creativity problem solving facilitator. Even though he was diagnosed with Multiple Sclerosis in 2008, he continues to help individuals, teams and organizations to enable effective thinking, problem solving, creativity, innovation, collaboration and teamwork. CEXINO consulting prides itself in helping organizations, small businesses and individuals establish innovation strategy and culture, build customer centricity, spark remarkability and enhance creative leadership. To find out more about Greg Z. Fainberg or CEXINO go to www.cexino.com for more information.

"Leave this world
a better place
than it was
when you
arrived in it"